T0052035

PRAISE FOR *OU1*

"Hillary's story of tragedy and triumphant return will inspire you."
JASON KOOP *Head coach for CTS-Ultrarunning, author of* Training
Essentials for Ultrarunning

"Hillary's story is blunt, raw, honest, and yet very positive and inspiring. I think anyone going through a rough time (accident, injury, depression, or simply just a low spot) would benefit from reading about Hillary's experience and how she was able to work her way back through the steps she took (both literally and figuratively), the mental challenges she overcame, and the new outlook she gained."
GINA LUCREZI *Professional ultra trail runner and founder of trailsisters.net*

"It wasn't her innate passion and talent for running that brought out the best version of professional athlete Hillary Allen. Rather, it was the horrific accident she experienced while doing it that did. By so candidly chronicling her recovery in Out and Back, Allen teaches us all that the progress of life isn't measured by one's physical transit through time or space but instead by the inner journey that accompanies us."
MEGHAN M. HICKS *Managing editor of iRunFar.com*

"Hillary Allen takes readers along an exciting and harrowing journey as she passionately tells her story about how she achieved enormous success, overcame a near-death experience, and then worked extremely hard to once again reach the mountaintop of success. Not only does she tell her story with fervor, but she also provides cues for the hard work, tenacity, and authenticity that has always defined her."
BRIAN METZLER *founding editor of* Trail Runner *magazine*

OUT

A RUNNER'S STORY OF SURVIVAL

AND

AGAINST ALL ODDS

BACK

HILLARY ALLEN

BLUE·STAR
PRESS

Published by Blue Star Press
PO Box 8835, Bend, OR 97708
contact@bluestarpress.com
www.bluestarpress.com

Book design and layout by Amy Sly
Illustrations by Claire Giordano

ISBN: 9781944515959

Printed in the United States

10 9 8 7 6 5 4 3 2

DEDICATION

To the dreamer, the go-getter, the defeated,
to anyone trying to navigate life's peaks and
valleys. Keep striving. Keep believing in
yourself. You're stronger than you realize.

CONTENTS

PROLOGUE

I n kindergarten, we had career day at school. We were told to pick something we wanted to be when we grew up and present it to the class. I wasted no time. I was ready. I hurried home and told my mother exactly what I needed.

First on the list was a lab coat. Next, we went to get the best and most realistic bug stickers from the craft store. I meticulously covered my new white lab coat with all the bug stickers I could fit on there. After that came my neon-orange bug net, and then finally—the biggest and most important piece of all—my bug collection. After practicing my presentation over and over, I marched right into that kindergarten classroom on career day declaring I wanted to get a PhD and be an entomologist—that's someone who studies bugs for a living.

I stayed on that academic path throughout my school years. And although my passion for bugs shifted from career to hobby, I built my future around pursuing a scientific career. I got a scholarship to a private liberal arts college to study chemistry, with my sights on graduate school. I accepted a PhD-candidate spot at the University of Colorado Denver, where I had plans to earn my doctoral degree in neuroscience and structural biology. I was in my element. I was doing it. I was making little kindergarten Hillary so proud.

But with all that work in the lab and countless hours at the lab bench, I had to find a way to reset. I needed a break and a way to let my mind rest. For me, recharging always revolved around movement. I had always been an athlete—how do you think I was able to catch all those bugs if I couldn't run around for hours? But my experience as an athlete was mostly in organized or team sports. My father and sister, on the other hand, were avid runners. I was attracted to the simplicity of running, as well as its efficiency—as a graduate student, I didn't have much time to waste. So, I found a local running group and started running a few days a week before heading into the lab.

Running, I discovered, helped my creative process. As a busy neuroscientist who spent many hours in the lab each day, I needed down time. I needed time to pause and let my mind wander and create, and ultimately become more productive. The more I worked, the more I wanted to run. Running became a sacred space: time warped, and I could just enjoy feeling free. After about three months running with this group, J'ne Day-Lucore, the organizer, introduced me to running on the trails. She had an impressive pedigree of trail running and wanted to share her passion. I became hooked, instantly.

No matter how stressful my day was, the time I spent running was my meditation. I was drawn in by the sounds of birds chirping, insects buzzing, and leaves rustling as the wind of my movement caressed the tree branches. I felt at one with nature. I could marvel at her beauty and complexity, especially at sunrise. There was something special about that time of day, greeting the morning, watching her wake up. Everything was still, quiet, and as the sun kissed the horizon, it felt like a secret shared between Mother Nature and me.

Running created a hallowed space. And I wanted more. More adventures, more traveling, more trails, more mountains, more challenges brought my way. I started designing my free time around running and began competing in trail races across the United States, traveling in any spare time from the lab and relishing every moment I got to lace up my shoes to run and explore.

I even picked up a nickname, coined by an ex-boyfriend who was also a training and adventure partner. He was an experienced ultrarunner who routinely did one-hundred-mile races, whereas I was a complete newbie who was just discovering how far she could go.

At the time, I was based outside of Golden, Colorado, and had only heard rumors of the myriad trails in Boulder, Colorado. Boulder boasted steep, technical, and brutal trails: a trail runner's paradise. It was a rite of passage to run those trails, and I planned to run there with my then boyfriend and a couple of his seasoned running friends.

We planned to do two steep peaks on the Boulder Skyline Traverse: Green Mountain and Bear Peak. I wasn't sure I could hang with them, but I told myself I'd hold on as long as I could, and when I got tired, I could just stop. Once we started on the trail, I discovered my rhythm and this wonderful thing called power hiking (a powerful hike that is more efficient on steep terrain when it becomes too steep or rocky to run). I got in a groove and before I knew it, I was at the top. I turned around to high five my friends, but when I looked back, no one was there.

For a few minutes I stood alone on the summit. It was a cool fall day, and I was surrounded by glimpses of golden and crimson leaves, preparing for the approaching cold of winter. It was my first winter running, and I still relished the sight of my breath fogging in the air as I exhaled. As I gazed out over the rolling hills that transitioned into the Rocky Mountains over the horizon, I started to wonder if I had made a wrong turn somewhere. Then I saw my friends coming up the trail, smiling and shaking their heads. My boyfriend said, "You're like a mountain goat! You're made for the uphill." Then he added, "I'm going to start calling you Hillygoat." The nickname has stuck ever since.

After being dubbed Hillygoat, I fittingly fell in love with a type of racing called "skyrunning." Sky races are super steep, gnarly, and technical, occurring on mountainous terrain that climbs and descends via the most direct route up and down the mountain. These races boast impressive elevation gain and usually involve some sort of off-trail traversing and scrambling. Skyrunning was made for me. In 2014, my first year of racing trails and ultras, I competed in the US Skyrunner Series. I won it.

Before long, my passion for running was conflicting with my lifelong goals and dreams of being a PhD scientist. With more course records and race results on my resume, I was getting attention from sponsors. One fall afternoon in 2014 I signed with The North Face between my neuroscience PhD seminar and conducting research experiments—and celebrated by dancing in the hallway outside my lab.

The following year, while still in graduate school, I started competing all over the world. It was the opportunity I had been waiting for, to really see where running could take me. To see if this, like science, was something I was destined to do. After competing in several international races in 2015, it hit me that for the first time in my adult life I felt like I had found what I was *made* to do.

Running made sense. It made more sense than anything else. My affinity for the natural world led me to science, but running gave me permission to get outside and really explore. Science might have allowed me to study the physical world, but running allowed me to experience it—to examine it with every fiber of my being and every one of my five senses. As a runner, I felt like the best version of myself. I was more creative, more productive. Running inspired me to accept more challenges—both on the trail and off. But I was conflicted. I had always wanted to be a scientist and earn my PhD, so I tried to do both—run, race, and travel while still pursuing my degree. But there weren't enough hours in the day, and my heart was continually pulled toward trail running. Something in my gut was telling me I couldn't let that opportunity go.

In the summer of 2015, I graduated with my master's degree in neuroscience, two years shy of a PhD. I cultivated a new life with trail running as the focus. I continued to teach chemistry, biology, and anatomy and physiology part-time at a small college, which gave me the flexibility to pursue my running career. My love of science encouraged my love for the trails and vice versa. I felt invigorated when I taught, and my time spent running made me a more vibrant, energetic, and engaging teacher. When school wasn't in session, I could spend extended time traveling, racing, and pursuing my other passions in running.

I was also able to encourage others to get active through outdoor recreation programs. I spoke at schools and events to encourage young girls and women to get out on the trails. I began working with more sponsors, collaborating on projects that felt like they meant something. I had the opportunity to run across Haiti to raise money for hurricane relief funds. I represented campaigns to raise money for clean air initiatives and education in schools. I felt like I was making a difference. Like I had a purpose.

But just as everything seemed to be falling into place, with one small step, my whole life changed. I was faced with the reality that I might never run or compete again, that my running career might be over.

This book is for anyone who has struggled through hardship or is struggling now. It's my testament to the power of never giving up or doubting the strength of the human spirit. It's about setbacks, resilience, and discovering beauty amid hardship. It's about fighting for yourself, embracing discovery, and not giving up when it seems like the only option.

In the pages that follow, I share my story of how I was able to rediscover myself while overcoming one of the greatest challenges of my life. I write about my continual process of survival and how I managed to keep fighting despite new obstacles.

I hope my story invites you to push yourself and dream bigger. I hope it motivates you to face head-on the struggles and challenges that threaten to break your spirit. But more than anything, I hope it inspires you to find your own inner strength and discover how to use setbacks as a way to uncover opportunities for growth—no matter the trial you may face.

WHEN MY PASSION NEARLY KILLED ME 1

In August of 2017, ranked number one in the world skyrunning circuit, I signed up for one of the hardest ultrarunning races in the world: the Tromsø Skyrace in Norway. Tromsø was one of my last races of the season and a dream opportunity for me. I had never been to that part of the world, and the competition gave me the chance to test my running in a way I never had before. It was also a way to explore a new place, by foot—my favorite method.

When race day came, I was motivated, inspired, and physically in top form. The odds were in my favor not only to complete the race, but to win. The weather that day was perfect. I felt great, and for the first three hours, I performed great. I was at my best. But as I climbed the most technical ridge on the course, a rock gave way. With one step I felt the ground give way beneath my feet—and the horizon turned upside down.

I was airborne.

I was falling off the edge of a cliff.

I felt the first impact, then the second, then the third.

I hit the ground again and again and again. With each impact, I felt bones breaking, skin ripping. I grasped for something, anything, to stop my momentum, but I didn't know which way was up, and as soon as I hit the ground I was spinning and airborne once again. I heard my own voice, floating somewhere above my head, declaring to me, calmly, "Hillary, this is it. You're dying."

This was my death.

Relax.

You've got to relax.

Breathe.

It will all be over soon.

I came to on the mountainside. Somewhere between the six points of impact and the 150 feet I had fallen, I lost consciousness. I remember the vivid pain when I came to. The world was throbbing, pulsing in and out. I couldn't see straight . . . only blurred shapes amid the blackout pain. I screamed out when the pain came, hoping that yelling would somehow release the intensity of the agony rushing over me. I felt like I was being suffocated. Unable to breathe or relax, I kicked my legs out of reflex and frustration. Then I thought to myself, *You're moving your legs; that's a good sign. You're not paralyzed.* But then the pain would rush back. I shut my eyes tight, and flashes of red and yellow danced across my eyelids. It hurt so much I had to stop moving.

Somehow, I realized, I was only in my socks. My shoes must have flown off my feet somewhere along the way down the mountainside, as I spiraled through the air like a tomahawk. I couldn't move my arms or hands, but tried to anyway. When I looked down, all I saw was a bundle of bones that didn't look like arms, and my wrists were turned the wrong way. There was so much blood. *What was happening?* I thought. *What had just happened?* I was confused, scared, and stranded—alone on the mountainside.

Suddenly there was a voice, and the face of another runner I vaguely recalled seeing earlier in the race. I had passed him as we ascended the steep part of the ridgeline, and we exchanged some words of encouragement. *Why was he here now? Had he fallen too?*

His arms were wrapped around me. His face was close to mine. *Had he been here the whole time?* He covered me with an emergency blanket—which was somehow still in the pack I was carrying—and later his jacket. He braced me and stayed with me, making sure I didn't fall any further down the mountainside.

Manu was his name, as I learned later. He had seen the rock fall, and me with it. Trained in first aid and wilderness responder training, Manu scrambled down the ridgeline after me.

Others had seen me fall too. My good friend Ian Corless, a professional photographer who worked for the Skyrunner World Series, was perched on the summit of the ridgeline waiting for my arrival, but as I came around the corner, what he saw through his lens wasn't what he expected. Another good friend, Martina Valmassoi, was with Ian. Martina, a professional ski mountaineer, runner, and photographer for the sporting goods company Salomon, was terrified when she saw me fall off the cliff. They both thought they had just witnessed my death. Panicked, they quickly called race director Kilian Jornet, who called the mountain rescue team. Martina, Ian, and Kilian scrambled their way down to me on the side of the mountain.

As I lay there, seeing the fear in their eyes, their features expressed what I was already thinking: *I'm dying.*

Martina put her puffy jacket over me, mostly to cover the blood but also to keep me warm. My body convulsed, either from pain, loss of blood, or shock—I couldn't tell which. I focused on Martina's voice as she stroked my head and told me it would all be OK. As I continued to cry out in pain, she looked to Ian and Kilian with worried eyes full of urgency, desperation, and despair.

Where was the rescue team?

After an agonizing thirty minutes, I heard the bellowing sound of the helicopter. As it approached, the vibrations of its blades and the wind created in its wake pulsed over me. The rescue operation was starting. A doctor lowered onto the ridgeline and scrambled down to me to assess the damage. "Inhale," he told me as he sprayed something up my nose, some sort of painkiller. It dulled the pain, but not my confusion. My eyes took in the shapes of their faces . . . they were still full of fear.

From that point on things moved quickly. There was a lot of movement. There was a lot of pain. Ian, Kilian, Manu, Martina, and the doctor tried to stabilize me. They shuffled rocks around, trying to make room to hoist me up onto the cot. The agony was unbearable. Any slight movement sent pain shooting throughout my body. With every movement, I yelled out in anguish, my cries eventually dissipating into a whisper. I didn't know where the pain was exactly. I couldn't pinpoint it or figure out where it origi- nated from—I felt it all over. As I was secured to the cot, the doctor fastened himself by my side and signaled to the helicopter pilot, who flew upward and outward from the side of Hamperokken Ridge. The feeling of falling swept over me again, and I closed my eyes tight.

Breathe. It will all be over soon.

Once inside the helicopter, I heard myself whimpering. The vibrations of the chopper sent pain signals pulsing throughout my body. I looked to the doctor and asked, tears streaming down my face, "Am I going to be OK?"

His eyes met mine, trying to comfort me, as he replied, "We're going to the hospital; they will take care of you."

Once we arrived at the hospital I was in and out of conscious- ness. Everything was fast-paced, and so many faces surrounded me, cutting off my clothes, peering into my eyes with lights, ask- ing me questions.

Could I move my legs or arms? Did I know who I was? Who was

my emergency contact? I remember reciting my mother's phone number and giving them her full name. I had to call her. One of the head doctors told me we would contact her soon, but first I needed X-rays and an MRI to assess my internal injuries. Time was of the essence. Tearfully I asked again, "Am I going to be OK?" She gazed at me and in her Norwegian accent said, "We are going to do the best we can."

When I came out of the MRI, that same doctor took my hand. Astonishment evident in her voice, she said, "We are so surprised, Hillary. You have no internal bleeding and your legs are not broken, but you need to go into surgery to clean out your wounds and fix your arms." I asked for my mother again, but there was no time. I was rushed off into surgery.

After surgery, back in the hospital bed, the memory of the accident played in my mind over and over again. Every time I started to drift off to sleep, I felt like I was spinning in the air, crashing into the side of the mountain. I saw the faces of the doctors who rescued me. I remembered the feeling of being airlifted, the doctor hanging off the side of the cot as I was hoisted up into the helicopter. And the pain, red, pulsing through me with the vibrations of the helicopter.

I didn't know if I was going to be OK. I didn't know how bad it was. And the fear of the unknown was almost as biting as the pain.

When I awoke after the initial shock and surgeries, I recounted my injuries. I had broken a total of fourteen bones—including my back (vertebrae L4 and L5 in multiple locations), multiple ribs, both wrists, and my feet—one badly sprained ankle, and a serious rupture of a ligament in the other foot. I also had a concussion, and too many lacerations to count.

The helicopter had transferred me to the nearest hospital, in Tromsø, Norway. That's where I lay in the hospital bed, unable to

I WAS STILL IN DENIAL. WHAT ACCIDENT? WHAT HAD HAPPENED? SOMEONE FELL? WHO FELL? WAS IT ME? WHY COULDN'T I MOVE? WHY WAS I THERE? I WAS SCARED AND ALONE.

move. Friends and other athletes from the race came to visit me, but it was all a blur. Drowning in the intense pain, and yearning for my mind to stop replaying the fall, I swam in and out of consciousness. When I called the nurse for more morphine, it wasn't to stop the pain, but rather to numb my thoughts—the warm rush that fell over my body allowed my mind to become quiet, and to drift off to sleep.

I don't remember much from those brief moments of consciousness or the faces who came to visit, or even what they said to me about the accident. I was still in denial. What accident? What had happened? Someone fell? Who fell? Was it me? Why couldn't I move? Why was I there? I was scared and alone. I hadn't been able to speak with my mother yet, or with anyone from home. Emelie Forsberg, a friend and co-race director with Kilian, told me she had spoken with her and she was on the way to see me.

I was scheduled for another surgery on my wrist the day my mother arrived at the hospital. When her face appeared in the doorway of my room, I broke down crying. The look in my mother's eyes—of fear, concern, sadness, and simultaneous relief—caused reality to crash over me. I knew, right then, it wasn't a dream. I was the one who had fallen, almost died, and yet somehow managed to survive.

The next few days were brutal. In an instant I had gone from being extremely fit and capable to utterly dependent. I couldn't move or even get out of my hospital bed. I was weak, I was in pain, and my spirit was broken. I hadn't moved from my bed in five days. My mother saw me slipping away into depression, wanting to give up. The nursing staff saw it too. I *was* giving up.

One day one of the nurses told me, quietly and frankly, "This isn't the end for you, Hillary. Now it's time to fight. It's time to move out of this bed. You are not done yet." She swung my legs over the side of the bed and practically carried me over to a chair in the shower, where she helped wash my body and hair. The exertion it took to move made me nauseous.

The next day, I decided to get out of bed to have breakfast in the chair next to my hospital bed. It probably took me thirty minutes to move there, with my mother's help. When the nurse came in and saw me sitting near the window, she smiled and took my vitals. My spirit wasn't completely broken yet. I started to try. Every day I did just a little bit more. I went on "walks" down the hospital corridors with my mother. We found rooms or patios where the sun streamed in, overlooking the fjords.

I stayed in the hospital in Norway for two weeks before I had the strength and medical clearance to fly home to Colorado. But traveling internationally with my injuries was no easy feat. I couldn't walk, and Tromsø doesn't have a very big airport, or planes large enough to accommodate wheelchair access. So, my mother talked to Maeve Sloane, my athlete manager with The North Face, who arranged for a private jet to fly to Tromsø and take me to an international airport.

The pilot of the private jet was nervous to take me, given my condition, and hired a medical assistant to accompany me on the flight. The assistant basically carried me on and off of the airplane. We flew into Munich, Germany, where a team of experts hoisted me onto a special chair built for handicapped passengers and carried me off the plane.

A wheelchair service waited for me inside the airport. I had a direct flight from Munich to Denver. It was my first time to fly first class on an international flight. Thankfully, I was able to lie down and rest in my big seat—in between taking painkillers and injections of blood thinners. I was overwhelmed with gratitude to Maeve and The North Face for arranging it all and getting me home safely.

Back in Colorado, I went straight to the doctor's office to reassess my injuries. First, I saw a hand specialist. After numerous X-rays, the doctor let me know that things weren't healing correctly. My left arm, which had rods and pins sticking out of it, was externally fixed. But my doctor wasn't happy with the status of the bone. He wanted to remove the hardware and put in a plate and screws internally to ensure proper healing. He told me if I continued healing as the bones were set now, I would have early arthritis and a limited range of motion.

I saw his point. So, I agreed to do the surgery. But he wasn't done. My right wrist was casted, with no hardware. It was healing, and the break wasn't as bad as the left wrist, but my doctor said that wrist needed surgery too—a plate and screws.

Two surgeries. He could do them on Thursday. It was already Tuesday. I needed a moment to think. I had never broken a bone before, never had major orthopedic surgery. I was overwhelmed. The doctor left the room to give me some time to consider.

A new doctor came in, Dr. Melissa Gorman. Her face told me everything I needed to know about her: stern, kind, no bullshit. She looked me straight in the eye and said she wanted to talk to me about my right foot.

There was an injury they missed in Norway, she said. A Lisfranc fracture. My mind was blank, as I'm sure was my face. I'd never heard of it. She took a deep breath and said, "Hillary, this is a *foot-changing* injury."

The Lisfranc is a ligament bridging the arch of the foot. It's a major ligament that contributes to the integrity of the foot, forming the arch, which is essential for standing, walking, and running. Lisfranc fractures are common in football, where players running at full speed are impacted from the side. Athletes who have surgery don't necessarily make a full recovery. She recommended—insisted—on surgery.

Time was crucial. It had already been two weeks since the rupture.

She told me it was unlikely I'd ever compete again.

All the feeling drained from my body.

The hand doctor came back into the room. He restated his diagnosis, impatiently waiting for my approval. I told him to do the surgery. "Good choice," he said as he nodded to his assistant to confirm the surgery date—Thursday. Then he exited the room and I looked to Dr. Gorman again. I knew I had no choice. My foot wasn't going to heal without the surgery, and if I ever wanted to get back to running, I at least had to try. I nodded to her, and we booked that surgery for the next day, Wednesday.

That night I couldn't eat. I couldn't speak. All I could do was stare, cry, hope—pray— that everything was going to be OK. I hardly slept. The few minutes of precious sleep I got were interrupted when I jolted awake with the dream of falling off that cliff in Norway. Tears came fast as, scared yet again, I relived the experience, the feeling of falling. Then I cried because I was thankful I was alive. And then the tears of fear came. Fearful of what was to come. My surgery, my recovery. Would I ever run again? I didn't know. The tears kept coming. The fear of the unknown was all-consuming.

My phone rang at 5:14 a.m. As I peeled my face off the damp pillow to look at my phone, I didn't recognize the number, but I answered it anyway.

"Hello," I said, tears already streaming down my face. The voice on the other end belong to Dave Mackey. A tremendous athlete, Dave was someone I looked up to, who had also suffered from a terrible accident.

Dave had fallen fifteen to twenty feet off Bear Peak, a summit I had run up often in my hometown of Boulder. But Dave's leg had been trapped under a rock, and after a year of recovery and rehab, he decided to amputate it. His story was incredible, his will was insatiable, and he was calling me the morning of my surgery to offer his encouragement and support.

"Hi Hillary, it's Dave. How are you doing?"

"Not good," I sputtered out, simultaneously laughing and crying.

"That's understandable," he said, chuckling as well. "I remember how scared I was before my surgery. I was a complete wreck! But these doctors know what they are doing, and they will do their best to take care of you. You'll be OK." Then he added, laughing, "Plus, they give you the good drugs, so you won't remember much of anything after that! Waiting is the worst part." Smiling a bit through the tears, I thanked Dave for calling. He wished me well and offered his support as we hung up.

Dave's unexpected pep talk gave me a little courage to face the day, and I started telling myself that I *would* be OK. That I would figure it out. I had the support of my family and my running community, and with that reassurance I started to foster belief in myself. I needed it for that first surgery. I prayed my doctor was ready and sharp and wouldn't screw up my foot with the screws she was putting in.

By 7 a.m. I was being prepped for surgery. Everything moved so fast. Nurses assessed the locations of all my injuries and breaks. They marked me up and told me they would remove my stitches while I was under anesthesia. My body looked like a coloring book that a child had gotten hold of: multi-colored marks all over, doctors' initials, and scribbled notes to make sure they operated on the correct foot (the right one).

I decided to get a nerve block for the pain. I watched as the anesthesiologist used an ultrasound to locate my peroneal nerve and stuck a needle in my leg. Within seconds, I could no longer feel my foot. A familiar face arrived: my surgeon, Dr. Gorman.

"Are you ready?" she asked.

Tears welling up in my eyes, I nodded. Her eye contact lingered, as if to tell me she had me now. It was her turn to do her job, and I could trust her. They wheeled me into the operating room. I gazed upward, blinking into the florescent lights as the world faded away.

The surgery lasted a couple of hours. It was late afternoon when I woke up from anesthesia. My eyes opened slowly. I was still in the hospital. Still in my hospital gown, with an IV in my arm. My mother, who had been sitting next to me, approached the bed to stroke my hair. My eyes were heavy with sleep, my body weighed down by the painkillers. Warm yet fuzzy, my senses were dulled. The doctor came in to tell us everything went according to plan.

My mother looked at me with tears in her eyes. "It's time to go home," she said as she kissed me on my forehead.

But it wasn't over yet. Tomorrow we'd go to another hospital for another set of surgeries. I closed my eyes wearily.

Back at my sister's house that evening, I was wheeled to the dinner table—a now-familiar routine. I hadn't eaten all day. And I wasn't hungry either. But I tried to eat—it was my only chance until the fasting period for the next day's surgery. Carefully, I placed my fork in my broken right hand and began strategically shoveling food into my mouth, instead of onto the floor. But as I ate, that pit in my stomach was still there. Food did nothing to fill it.

I was exhausted from the day's events, the emotional stress and trauma of the operation. But I couldn't sleep. Again, I just lay there. Restless, I texted Dave Mackey. Told him the first surgery went well and that I was preparing for two more the next day, on my wrists. I was afraid, unsure, and overwhelmed by the thought of another operation. Dave offered his support, and sometime around 2 a.m. I dozed off.

Day two was the same routine, with teams of doctors and nurses and anesthesiologists swarming around me, marking me up, and asking me questions. But I didn't cry. This time, I was quiet. Numb. I wanted it all to be over. As I drifted off, my hand surgeon gave me a warm smile and reassuring nod.

Waking up on the second day of surgery was different. A nerve block hadn't been possible for this procedure, so I woke with a dull ache that overpowered the painkillers. That faint ache grew into deep pain as I become more lucid after the surgery, and it persisted throughout the night. No amount of painkillers could touch the pain. Whimpering, I cried myself to sleep out of pure exhaustion, only to awaken within an hour, my arms throbbing, as if someone held a tuning fork to my wrist, the vibrations rippling the fresh hardware inside. I counted down the minutes until I could take another painkiller. Time seemed to move in reverse.

I had hit rock bottom. I was defeated. Completely broken and rebroken. This was my reality. I could hardly do anything for myself. Helpless and hopeless, I faced complete and utter dependency. But in that moment, I knew I had a choice: give up or fight.

I could accept my fate and lie idly by, passing the time waiting for my body to heal—hoping that it would. This was the easier choice, the less painful one. The alternative was to question the impossible and challenge what the doctors thought was possible—challenge what even I thought was possible.

Every day was a humbling new experience, and I never knew what to expect. Some days were excruciating. I felt trapped by the slow progress, the constant pain, the loss of identity and motivation, and the doubts about my future. I had no idea where my life was heading, or if I would overcome these injuries that threatened to consume my joy and the very essence of who I was. Every day I asked myself these questions, and every day I knew I had to face them. I knew I had to try.

WHY AM I ALIVE?

I'm angry. Filled with despair, grief, and an incredible

sense of hopelessness, helplessness. I hate myself; I

feel worthless. These thoughts are weighing on me

constantly, an incessant nagging, cementing me in the

depths of self-loathing.

—JOURNAL ENTRY, AUGUST 2017

After my accident, I was thankful to be alive, surprised even, but that wasn't the only emotion I experienced. I was also angry. Really angry. Why was I alive? Why did this happen to me? With all my technical experience and knowledge of the mountains, my skill level and expertise, why did this accident happen to me? I was at the top of my sport, the best in the world, and this happened to *me?!*

I was bitter. Confused. Running had made me feel whole and complete. And it had been ripped away from me in an instant, with just one small step. *Why me?* I couldn't answer that question, which infuriated me even more. The potential end of my career loomed large—and it was something I was unwilling to accept or admit.

As a professional athlete, I had built a career on being capable, strong, and competent in my own body. And I excelled because I had always been such a strong-willed, "do-it-yourself" person. If I wanted to buy something I couldn't afford, I'd get a second job (or a third), until I got what I wanted. If I didn't get the grade I desired on a test (usually anything less than 100 percent), I'd spend more time studying until I mastered every inch of the material. That's how I approached life, and it's how I approached being an athlete too.

I've never been someone who desired the easy way out. I value hard work, and I believe that if I don't get the outcome I want, it's because I didn't work hard enough. This ethic has value. It creates a sense of accomplishment after working hard to achieve a job well done—especially since I made it happen myself. But that internal validation and pride in my ability to do everything myself became an obstacle as I faced new challenges in my recovery.

Not only was I frustrated by my inability to work my way out of my current predicament, I was also upset over my loss of independence. I couldn't do *anything* myself. Remember, I had broken fourteen bones: five ribs, vertebrae L4 and L5 in my back, both feet (multiple bones in each), and both bones in both of my lower arms. To say I was limited is an understatement. Of course, I couldn't do everything myself; I needed help, and lots of it.

I required a constant chaperone and people to check in on me. Each morning I woke up and enjoyed the solitude for a few sweet moments as I did an assessment of my body. I looked over all my casts and cuts. *Yep, I'm still injured*, I'd think to myself. Then I would take a deep breath as I read the messages on my phone, preparing myself for the day to come.

Today was Michelle's turn to meet me for coffee. Michelle was a friend from Skratch Labs who routinely checked in on me. I assessed my pain level and motivation level. *Pain, at about an 8,* I thought to myself. *Motivation, probably at a 0, or -1. Can a 10-point scale go negative? It does today.* I took a deep breath. *I don't want to go out today.* But I knew that even if I canceled, Michelle would still come check on me. I took another deep breath. I had managed to not get up in the middle of the night, but my knee scooter was there next to my bed just in case. I eyed the scooter. I needed to go to the bathroom.

I began to pry myself out of bed, using my elbows and butt to scoot to the edge. It was 7:45 a.m. Michelle would be there at 8. Finally, I made it onto my scooter, but I didn't have the energy to put on my clothes yet. Wearing just my underwear, I scooted to the bathroom.

A knock sounded at the door as Michelle used the spare key to get into my apartment. Was it 8 a.m. already? I left the bathroom door open and glanced at the clock as I made my way back to my bedroom. 8:04 a.m. Michelle helped me get dressed and get out the door. Making it down the street for coffee was my only goal.

My privacy was gone, and I constantly needed assistance. I'm someone who needs her space. Her freedom. It's part of me, as if the name Hillary itself means maverick. But I was stripped of my independence, my routine, my strength, and—in my opinion—my self-worth. I no longer felt capable. I no longer felt strong. Everything was out of my control, and I couldn't work my way out of it. I wanted things to change, but I saw no way out. How was I supposed to recover from my injuries and keep moving forward when I couldn't even take care of myself?

Desperate, I tried to find small tasks I could do—anything—to feel useful and somewhat capable. After the surgeries to place metal plates in my arms, I couldn't lift anything heavier than a twelve-ounce beverage. Everything was too heavy. I couldn't even cook, which was something I loved to do. I couldn't grasp a spatula, let alone hold a utensil in my hand. Unable to bear having someone feed me, I decided to duct tape a piece of foam around my fork to create a grip big enough for me to grasp.

Life didn't stop after my surgeries. I had many obligations and appointments. The list of things I had to do kept piling up in my head: physical therapy, the grocery store, work, doctors' appointments. But I couldn't do any of it alone.

Today was a shower day. It had been three days, at least, since my last shower. I didn't think I smelled too bad, but I was beginning to feel grimy and my hair was greasy. My designated person for the day was there to help me. It didn't matter at this point who it was; the routine was simple. Help me undress, remove my casts, and make sure I don't fall: that was all they needed to do. There was a walker in the shower, placed strategically so I could lean my elbows on it as I balanced on one foot. I scooted up to the walker and transferred my weight onto it. Then my helper for that day turned on the water and helped me bathe. We got me dressed and into bed, exhausted, about forty-five minutes later.

The worst part of my dependency was not the embarrassment of having my mother, sister, or friends see me naked as they helped me go to the bathroom or wash my hair and body. The worst part was the completely raw vulnerability.

Physical nakedness was fine, but my state of weakness and dependency made me feel exposed down to my core—like the weakest part of me was on display under blinding, fluorescent lights. It wasn't the shower that exposed me; it was the vulnerability of having to ask, yet again, for help getting dressed and undressed.

One night I wake up exhausted. It's 2:05 a.m. *Did I ever fall asleep?* My foot, back, and ribs throb as I try to get comfortable. My arms hurt. As my frustration mounts, warm tears flow down my cheeks, into my ears, and onto my pillow.

"I can't do this anymore," I say aloud. *I wish the accident had killed me. This is too hard. I can't do this. How am I supposed to get through another day? I don't see a point to life. I don't see any reason to keep going. Can I do this? How will I do this?* I woke up a few hours later, my face pressed against a wet pillow. Somehow, I had fallen back asleep, drained by grief and despair.

Many athletes who struggle with injury feel a sense of loss when they aren't able to train or move in the ways to which they are accustomed. It's more than the loss of the physical act of sport; it's a profound loss of self. Feelings of worthlessness accompany injuries, which only makes the injuries themselves worse.

Grief and loss weigh heavy on the human heart. They are the unwelcome guests of depression, job change, a breakup, moving, divorce, a midlife crisis, or—in my case—loss of a passion. I was separated from what I loved, something that truly made me feel whole, complete, and a part of this world. I felt like I had lost myself, my purpose in everyday life, and my direction and reason to keep going every day.

Despite my frequent thoughts of despair and the overwhelming desire to give up, I found the smallest reasons to keep going. Sometimes it was my coach, Adam St. Pierre, coming to check up on me or bring me to my physical therapy appointment. Other times it was the desire to feel the sun warm my skin while I sat on a bench across the street from my apartment. These reasons to keep going, even amid the dark thoughts of giving up, prevailed. I think I knew, deep down, it would all pass, and if I let myself give up, I would never forgive myself. I had to keep working at it.

The mental side of recovery was the biggest challenge I faced early on, and it still remains an obstacle today. My physical body had been broken, but the depression and mental obstacles I was forced to overcome . . . these were things I was not prepared for.

My significant injuries and the obstacles I faced every day—showering, eating, moving around—were problems I could work through. The real challenge was within my headspace, my thoughts—places where I could get stuck. That's where the real battle of survival began.

I routinely journaled about feeling hopeless and helpless, listing the reasons why I wished the accident had killed me instead. Death seemed like an escape from the emotional challenges that confronted me. It was an escape from feeling trapped by my immobility, trapped in dependency, trapped by self-deprecating thoughts that made me feel worthless and purposeless, without meaning or direction.

When I confided in friends, they were surprised and confused by these dark emotions. Why wasn't I just grateful to be alive? They didn't understand. They couldn't understand, because they hadn't experienced the immense grief that comes with losing your sense of self or the thing you love so much that it has become not just a part of you; it *is* you.

But expressing these emotions was important. Experiencing the extreme lows, and being honest with the people in my life, up-front with how I was feeling . . . this was key to moving through my dark emotions. As much as I wanted to deny the existence of such dark thoughts and put on a happy face, smile through the pain, and express only gratitude for my survival, it wouldn't have been genuine. It wouldn't have been real. I didn't feel that way. I allowed myself the space to stand in my truth, the courage to admit I was angry, and the freedom to express my grief and despair, while thinking of death as an escape from the state I was enduring.

Being honest with myself about how I was really feeling is what saved my life and put me on the path to survival.

Eventually, help became easier to accept. I started to realize there wasn't weakness in needing or accepting help. In fact, there was a beauty to it. Requiring help and receiving it from others created close relationships that would not have existed otherwise. The people in my life who were selfless enough to help me also gave me a sense of belonging, told me that I mattered, and showed me that I was part of a community that cared about me. Help was a gift provided by those near to me. I found out who my people were. Allen Lim was one of them.

From the moment I started running professionally, Allen was there. I met him early on in my running career at a food truck in Leadville, Colorado. His company, Skratch Labs, was one of the nutrition sponsors for the race. We started chatting and instantly hit it off. Allen, a brilliant physiologist, could not only throw down science knowledge but was witty, funny, and super down to earth.

Not long after meeting him, I became a Skratch Labs athlete and our friendship grew. He came to various race events and multiple The North Face athlete summits. He even guest-lectured in the anatomy and physiology classes I taught part-time at Front Range Community College outside of Boulder. Allen was one of the first to visit when I came home from Norway. His gift to welcome me home was a bidet toilet kit to ease my limitations in the bathroom. Yep, Allen and I were really close.

Shortly after my surgeries in Denver, I was ready to move back to my home in Boulder. But first I had to determine if I could stay in my apartment. Allen brought me back to Boulder and took me to meet an in-home nurse who would help me with daily tasks several times a week.

When we got to my apartment, I was immediately faced with the first two steps leading up to the porch. As Allen and the nurse looked on, I got on my butt and used my elbows to push myself up the stairs, then worked my way up to lean against my walker and scooter. I eventually got indoors, where I had to climb another flight of stairs to my room.

Then I had to test getting into the bathroom—where there was yet another step. I was trying to prove to myself that I could live in my apartment and establish some sort of a routine on my own, and it was exhausting. *I can do it*, I kept telling myself. But the truth was, I couldn't.

The nurse and Allen patiently watched me struggle, then finally sat me down and told me this wasn't a possibility. I needed to find another place to live.

That was the moment I realized how extraordinary it can be to accept help from someone, how it's not really about me at all. It's really about the process of giving help and receiving it. My community grew because I was in a place of need. Over time, I realized I was the only one who felt uncomfortable, as the receiver of help. No one who helped me saw me as weak or insignificant. And none of them asked for anything in return.

That day Allen offered his house to me. While I stayed in his guest bedroom, he cooked wonderful meals for me, supported me, joked with me, and gave me a shoulder to lean on as I hopped one-footed down the stairs in and out of his apartment complex. He believed in me, and I started to believe in myself.

While I searched for a more permanent place to live for a couple months, my community continued to show up for me. Two of my friends—Rush and Julia, a married couple I'd known since moving to Boulder—offered me a room in their house. It was on the ground floor, and Julia even built a ramp over their two front steps to allow me easy access into their home. I stayed there for two months, graciously accepting their generosity and hospitality.

Allen, my team at Skratch Labs, Rush, and Julia weren't the only ones who demonstrated the power of community. I had many friends around the world who also offered to help, some of whom I didn't even know. They reached out via Instagram or social media, sending care packages or offering words of encouragement. I became pen pals with people as we shared recovery stories and encouragement. I grew to realize that being vulnerable and needing help made me feel strong, like I had a purpose. It allowed me to delve deeper into the meaning of life: why I was here, and what I hoped to accomplish and live for in the future.

Being extremely vulnerable and honest with my grief, anger, and despair allowed me to be present in each moment, accept where I was at that moment, confront my crazy emotions, and find a way through. Accepting help gave me purpose each day and allowed me to see the reasons why I must keep trying, living, and recovering, no matter how defeated I felt.

The valuable process of being vulnerable not only let me connect with others, but also grew my belief in myself. Early in the healing process most days still felt impossible, and I often had the urge to give up. But, gradually, I started to lean into my vulnerability. Even on the days when I didn't want to keep going—especially on those days—I still got out of bed, tucked my journal and wallet in my basket, and found a way to get out the door so I could scoot my way to my favorite coffee shop, Spruce Confections.

My morning routine became a ritual, a deliberate choice I made to challenge the voice telling me to give up. Sometimes that voice would whisper in my ear the entire mile-long scoot down to the coffee shop. But somewhere between the coffee, the outdoor patio, and the baristas—who soon knew me by name—those negative thoughts would settle to the back of my head and I could find peace for a moment.

Rather than ignore those negative thoughts, it was important for me to engage with them, to question them and ask them what their purpose was. I started journaling every day, taking note of my mood and motivation level, asking myself how frustrated I was and how much I wanted to fight. It was quite incredible how my feelings varied day to day, or even throughout the day.

I knew from past experience that pushing through or ignoring uncomfortable emotions only made them worse or manifested them in bigger, uglier ways. I wasn't going to pretend the negative thoughts weren't there. I wanted to understand them, be compassionate with myself, and find a way to heal.

One way I did this was by starting a list of affirmations. A list I earmarked in my journal so I could easily flip back to the page and read them out loud to myself. Not only when I was feeling good, but also—and more important—when I started to doubt the process or felt like my negative thoughts were drowning me.

I choose to live my life from my beliefs—especially my most positive beliefs toward my best behaviors to create great feelings, not the other way around.

I am worthy. I have worth. It's more worth than defined by my running, or being an athlete . . . it's in my mind, my essence, my smile, my heart, my being. It's within myself, in every part of me.

Reading and rereading these affirmations became an important part of the healing process for me. I still read my affirmations today, not just to promote recovery or change, but to take care of myself and cultivate a healthy perspective and mindset for dealing with adversity.

I wrote a lot of affirmations about my injuries and recovery too. Reading them helped me remember it was a process; it wouldn't happen overnight, and there was a reason for all my suffering if I consciously made the choice to engage with it.

This will make me better. I will let this make me better.

I am the mighty one! I choose hard, for everything hard makes me better.

I understand that the mind follows the body and the body follows the mind. Each day and each moment I will take care of both.

I am better than a result. I am better than the past or how it defines me.

Despite the challenges of my injuries, I am certain that my best physical and mental days are ahead—that being the best athlete I can ever be is only possible because of the challenges I face now. Believe.

That last affirmation got me through a lot of hard times. It allowed me to come face to face with the darkest emotions and confront them.

Every day I confronted fear: fear of never being a professional athlete again, fear of never doing what I loved, fear of my recovery process, fear of being in pain forever, fear of having to compromise my dreams or who I was as a person. Fear consumed me, swallowing me up. So, I started writing out my frustrations, giving them the space they deserved, and then I would flip back to my affirmations and start reading. Slowly, as I read through the list, I started to find my strength again. I would read that final affirmation a couple of times, take a deep breath, and carry that belief with me throughout the day, or at least the next hour, when I needed to be reminded again of my worth and purpose.

3 JUST KEEP SHOWING UP

Just keep showing up. This was a mantra early in my recovery. In the beginning, there were days when my motivation to train was low, when it was hard to get out the door. But there was also the feeling when it all fell away and things suddenly clicked, when I had problem-solved my way through the lack of motivation and the thoughts holding me back. I took this feeling, this memory, into my recovery and told myself to keep showing up. If I kept showing up, I believed, something good would come of it, and I would feel differently on the other side.

I reminded myself of this constantly. When I didn't want to do my boring physical therapy exercises, I told myself that something good would come out of it if I did. Those exercises had a purpose. Even if it wasn't a perfect day, a perfect routine, even if it felt like shit, it was progress. It was something. And it all contributed to a bigger picture. Imperfectly perfect.

In my head, I pictured myself building a brick house. I was at the beginning of the process, building the foundation, laying each brick by hand and adding the next—methodically placing it and cementing it to its neighbor. If one brick dented or chipped or had a little crack in it, I didn't care. I placed each imperfect brick in the foundation, because next to the others the flawed brick becomes stronger, reinforced, better.

Each brick was like a day in my recovery. I was building something; I just couldn't yet see what it was. Each piece was contributing to a bigger picture and a greater story. Doing the work and showing up each day, laying each brick, gave me hope that I was building a strong foundation for a beautifully imperfect home.

My bones would take time to heal—ten weeks before I could bear weight with my arms, back, and feet. The operation in my right foot was worse. The ligament I fractured would take a long time to repair. I wouldn't be able to bear weight on that foot for three months. That meant no walking or driving—except, of course, for my knee scooter, which got me around my apartment or Rush and Julia's house. It wasn't so good on stairs, though. Any time I encountered steps, I got down on my butt and did the "butt scoot"—a very technical term—up or down the stairs. The tricky part was getting back on my foot and onto my scooter once I reached the bottom or top. But every time I did, I thought of the bricks I was laying.

My immediate future seemed to move rather slowly. Instead of planning my weeks and months around my next race or event, I focused on the immediate future—on the moment or hour in front of me, and how I could navigate those moments and show up in my best form, having faith that if I strung enough moments together, they would add up to some form of progress that I could look back on and measure. So, I started to form new goals, ones that didn't focus solely on racing or traveling or a training block. I decided to hyper-focus on what I could do for my recovery each day, and be diligent in showing up in the present moment.

I also wanted to keep my life as routine as possible, to give me a sense of normalcy. Of course, for me, that involved some sort of movement. Since I wasn't able to do much, especially in the first several months, I focused on what I could do—a lot of physical therapy. I focused on strengthening the muscles I *could* use, doing non-weight-bearing exercises on the ground to activate my glutes, inner and outer legs, back, and core.

Every morning at 5 a.m. my friend Rush and I made our way down the stairs to the garage, where he had built a home gym, to do our respective workouts. We had a system. I waited by the front door while he took my scooter down to the garage, then came back upstairs. I'd put one arm around his shoulders and hop down the stairs as I leaned on him. Once in the gym, I would plop on the floor to do my leg lifts and non-weight-bearing physical therapy exercises for an hour while he did his own workout. We'd blare music, talk, and laugh. Not only was it a wonderful start to the day, having a plan helped me stay focused and get out of bed. It wasn't much, and I never broke a sweat, but it was something. A routine I could feel accomplished about.

There was a routine after the gym too: coffee, shower, break-fast, and then more coffee. These little tasks also gave me purpose. Rush and I would race to see who could get back upstairs first. I was rather slow at first, taking off and putting back on my removable wrist casts, precariously stumbling into furniture as I moved around my bedroom, trying to get dressed. Rush would yell from the room next door to make sure I was alright. But I got better and faster with time. I got used to a slow routine, meticulous in my movements, calculated and precise, and not rushing the process. Drinking coffee after I had safely showered and dressed myself was a reward well worth the slow process. Eventually, I even enjoyed the routine of my brokenness. I liked how the slow pace brought me into the present moment.

It was all a matter of perspective—a deliberate one at that. I was forced to keep showing up, no matter my mood or lack of motivation. It was a wonderful practice to allow myself to be imperfect, to show up when I wasn't feeling my best, and to learn to accept help from others, literally leaning on them when I couldn't stand on my own or I lacked strength to face the day. I didn't have to be perfect, or "strong" or "together." I just had to be me. Healing, flawed, as I was—as I am.

This perspective helped me find my way back to my other passion: science. When I was injured and couldn't run, I had extra energy and curiosity and a need to explore, so I leaned into science more. The school year was starting again, and so was my part-time job teaching chemistry, biology, anatomy and physiology, and other general science classes at Front Range Community College outside Boulder. I had started the job before the accident, and I felt it was important to return to maintain some sense of routine and normalcy in my life.

One short week after my second series of operations—just three weeks after falling off that cliff—I was back in the classroom teaching. I vividly remember that first day back. Even getting to the classroom was no small feat.

Since I couldn't drive, I started using the car service Via Mobility, which was handicap accessible. The first day, I scooted up to the driver, Fred, as he pulled up to my doorstep at 7:45 on a Monday morning. He was bright and happy as he lowered the ramp down from the van for me to enter. I felt embarrassed for a moment that I needed this service just to get to work. It felt excessive. But the bus took too long and the schedules were inconvenient. Every day I made the call to reserve my rides to and from work, and when the car service wasn't running (usually after my night class) I'd call my mom or my dad to take me home.

I was nervous that first morning in the van as I headed back to the college. I had taught many classes before, but on that day, I felt different. I had so many questions. Would the students respect me when I pulled up on a scooter to class? Would they take me seriously or get annoyed with how long it took me to move around and do things? I had my same scientific knowledge and ability to teach, but still, I was scared. I had none of my usual confidence. Fred could tell I was distracted. He kept asking me questions about my accident and injuries, but I wasn't willing to reply with the full details of my story. I felt impatient. I just wanted to get to my class.

We pulled up to my building at 8:12 a.m. I was early. Class didn't start until nine, but I wanted to make sure everything was prepared when the students arrived. A security guard, Dan, waited for me at the front door and escorted me to my classroom. My boss had informed him of my arrival so he could assist me in getting to class. It was nice to have him there, opening doors for me and limiting the inquiries I got from people as I scooted by. Once Dan had dropped me off in my classroom and said, "Call me if you need me," I closed the door and started to prepare. I looked around. Nothing had changed. I went about my normal pre-class routine: first, power on the computer and projector, then review my copy of the lecture, even though I already knew the topic by heart.

Even with the logistical stress and my fears about teaching again, I couldn't find an excuse to stop showing up. With everyone else showing up for me, how could I not keep showing up for myself, no matter my disabilities, injuries, or emotional or mental state that day? Each obstacle could be overcome. I just had to find a solution—and there's always a solution. It may take a little extra time and a little more patience, but there's always a way through.

As I showed up for myself each day, I also showed up for others, and they, in turn, showed up for me. This was an extremely rewarding lesson. While I continued to show up for my students, they showed up for class engaged and eager to learn. I was teaching and leading through example. Nothing in my chemistry book could have taught me that.

That semester I taught integrated science, an introductory course that covered both chemistry and physics. It was one of my favorite classes, the perfect blend of two of the best subjects in science. The first chapters were about Newton's laws, mapping out the rules of the larger physical world and how it moved before delving into the subatomic world of chemistry. I realized that in these early topics I had an interesting opportunity—I could apply the details of my accident to generate real-life examples and applications to those scientific laws of motion.

Newton's first law: an object in motion will stay in motion unless acted upon by another force. In the case of my fall, I would have kept running and staying in motion, but that pesky rock gave way underneath my foot, changing my momentum and therefore my path of motion. Another force had acted upon me.

Newton's second law: $F = ma$, in which "F" is the force, "m" is the mass, and "a" is the acceleration due to gravity. Basically, this describes the motion of an object as a "force," dependent on its mass and acceleration. A simple example I used was to calculate the force of my body hitting the ground, given my mass and acceleration due to gravity (which is a constant 9.81 m/s^2). I had a lot of force.

Newton's third law: to every action there is an equal and opposite reaction. Most textbooks use the example of swimming to demonstrate this law. It's not a bad example; this law is why you can "pull" on water and that force you put into the water is "given" back to you by the water itself, propelling you forward. I, however, liked my example of breaking bones. When I fell off that ridgeline and hit the ground, the force I exerted onto the rocks—the force I had calculated in Newton's second law—was "given" back to me. Some of that force my body could absorb, say as bruises or damaged blood vessels, but there was too much force left over for my body to absorb. That leftover force caused my bones to break. This example, a quite visual one, was something the students could remember.

From my own perspective, these examples were important. They allowed me to be honest, to show up as I was, and to keep showing up throughout the semester, even on those days when I felt like shit, when I felt not good enough, when I was in pain, when I was tired. I just kept showing up. Doing so was adding up to something bigger, and the students could see it too. They were encouraged to keep asking questions and to keep studying, even if the material was new and difficult for them. We played off one another.

The second course I taught that semester was anatomy and physiology. Perfect, right? The first day of class I rolled in on my scooter, sporting all my casts, with the textbook and a laptop in the front basket. The students were surprised I was their teacher. "Wait, are you supposed to be here?" one of them asked. When I told him I was his teacher, his eyes got big. He apologized and sat down in his seat.

I started class by recounting my accident to explain why I looked the way I did. Then we moved on to our first lesson: a review of my injuries. Not in a storytelling kind of way, but rather in an instructional way—I assigned the students the task of correctly identifying all my broken bones on the classroom skeleton, Karl, using correct anatomical vocabulary to locate and describe the nature of each break. We did this exercise for my ligament injuries too. Not a single student got that question wrong on the following exam.

Teaching helped me begin to find my self-worth again, outside of running. This part of me was always there—I always had these interests—but I was rediscovering them, learning to appreciate them more. Following the adage "just keep showing up," I was also discovering my own internal strength, curiosity, and commitment. I learned to keep going, to never give up despite every obstacle along the way. Instead, I slowed down, shifted my perspective, and believed in the process.

NOT BEING ABLE TO RUN WAS DEVASTATING, AND THE FEAR SURROUNDING MY RETURN WAS DEBILITATING, BUT IT ALSO FORCED ME TO TAKE IT EASY, LOOK AT SITUATIONS DIFFERENTLY, AND SEEK OUT NEW WAYS TO ENGAGE WITH MYSELF.

Not being able to run was devastating, and the fear surrounding my return was debilitating, but it also forced me to take it easy, look at situations differently, and seek out new ways to engage with myself. In the process, I learned more about myself and grew in my other interests and passions. It was a necessary slowdown. A necessary stop for me and my life. I've wondered many times why this accident happened to me, and although I couldn't come up with a definitive or satisfying explanation, the main takeaway I could justify was to see it as an opportunity—for growth, for learning, for patience. An opportunity to trust myself, to learn what I was made of, what I was capable of, and how one of the most horrible experiences of my life could teach me to become a better version of myself.

Competition and hard work have always appealed to me. I've always liked hard things, and I like finding a way to push through them. Once I put my mind to something, it's happening. It's just a matter of when.

I remember my first fifty-mile race. It was the summer of 2014 (three years before the accident) and I was terrified. I had run fifty-kilometer (thirty-one-mile) races before, but I didn't know what would happen to myself—or my legs—after the fifty-kilometer mark. Even though I trained hard for the race, nothing can prepare you for the unknown. You just have to go for it.

When my alarm sounded at 3:30 a.m., I was sleeping in a tent on damp grass outside the recreation center in Dayton, Wyoming. The rustling of sleeping bags and clattering dishes in the tents next to me broke the early-morning quiet. I turned on my headlamp to find my lighter and fire up the Jetboil so I could make coffee and breakfast before 4 a.m., when I would catch the bus to the starting point of the race. The race would start somewhere fifty miles away, in the Big Horn Mountains Wilderness in Wyoming.

As I started the race, my motto of "one step at a time" ran through my head. My plan was to take everything as it came and problem-solve my way through any situation that presented itself.

The race started in the dark. I headed down the road, which lead to a single-track trail, surrounded by silhouettes and bobbing headlamps behind and ahead of me. The route began downhill, a gradual descent over the first fifteen miles. I started out conservatively, focusing not on the women passing me but on my breathing and my footsteps, eating and drinking as I ticked off each mile and each aid station. I had studied the course profile and knew generally when the big climbs were coming, so I was prepared for them, but I wasn't prepared for all the bathroom pit stops I made in those first miles. Apparently, Folgers instant coffee made in a tent isn't the most polite on the stomach. I had to stop and poop in the bushes about five times in those first fifteen miles. I wanted to problem-solve and that's what I was getting: how to poop as fast as possible and as discreetly as possible. After each pit stop, I tried to stay calm and focus on my mantra: "one step at a time."

To my surprise, my strategy worked. I was chasing down first place and nearing the fifty-kilometer mark. Standing next to my father at this aid station, my mother wore on her face the emotions of my mind. Her eyes were wide, concerned, excited; she seemed in awe that I was doing so well. She and my father screamed words of encouragement as I stuffed a watermelon wedge and a potato into my running pack and stepped off into the unknown. My mother's anxious look was stamped into my brain, but I felt no fear or apprehension, just anticipation. *Let's go!* I told myself. *We'll see what happens after fifty kilometers!*

As the remaining twenty-two miles ticked by (this fifty-mile race was actually a fifty-three-mile race), I felt committed to the uncertainty and the unknown. My memory of my course profile had left me by this point, like I was going blind—the climbs became steeper, longer, and more exposed to the sun. My legs weren't giving up, even though my mind seemed to be wavering. So, I kept going.

As I climbed each hill, I focused on one step at a time until eventually the hill peaked, which left me wondering when the downhill would end, and the perpetual pounding of my quads would subside. But my legs didn't stop, so I didn't let my mind stop either.

I played games with my mind, counting my footsteps, singing a song, or picking out the sounds of the cicadas and locusts as I passed through each meadow.

Finally, I reached the last aid station. I had run forty-eight miles, with five miles to the finish. I had made it that far and successfully solved all the obstacles to get there, and to my astonishment, my legs were fine. They hadn't fallen off, and they still felt responsive and relatively normal. I took off from the aid station, anxious for the finish line. That's when it hit me.

I bonked; I hit the wall.

Without warning, I started crying. It wasn't because of my legs—they were still fine. It was all in my mind. The last five miles suddenly seemed impossible. I couldn't wrap my mind around still having that far to go. In retrospect, it seems so silly. I had already run forty-eight miles! What was another measly five? But in the moment, that didn't matter. I was losing it.

My brain raced for a solution, some game to play. *Should I count my steps? My breath? Should I talk to someone? Should I talk to myself?* I choked out, "Hillary, you can do this—just keep moving!"

Just as I finished saying this out loud, I passed another runner along the road. He was eating M&M's, and the smell of chocolate wafted over. Instantly I knew what I needed: FOOD! That's why I was bonking and losing motivation. I was hungry—hangry, most likely.

Thankfully, there was one last aid station on the road, where a group of volunteers had gathered to help in the final miles of the race. I had energy gels, but even the thought of them made me gag. But this guy had M&M's! I grabbed a handful, said thank you, and started running down the road again. As soon as I put a few of those wonderfully sweet and warm M&M's in my mouth, it felt like rocket fuel. I don't think my legs moved any faster, but my mood instantly improved. I felt upbeat again! But that happy feeling didn't last long; my body was working so hard that those blissful M&M's only kept me happy for about five minutes. This tearful, unmotivated hangry phase happened about seven more times in those last five miles of the race, each bout of "hanger" resolved by some more M&M's. It was comical, but I learned something that day about what my body could endure without quitting, and how my mind and body were linked. I had to listen to the signs, find a solution, and learn to take care of both in the moment. One step— and one M&M—at a time.

During the low points of my recovery process, I'd often reflect on moments like these—and the metaphorical last five miles of the race—when I was frustrated with my physical therapy exercises or bored of the gym and its confining walls. I would relive that first fifty-mile race, or one of my hard "character-building" runs, as I had dubbed my toughest practice runs. I'd reach for that feeling of trying hard, of leaning into the uncomfortable feelings, the frustration in my mind, or the fatigue in my legs—the feeling of wanting to quit. Then I'd put one foot in front of the other, like I always had, and keep moving forward.

My building was going up brick by brick, but it wasn't finished. Sometimes it felt like building that metaphorical foundation would never be complete, but I kept showing up for myself, for my recovery, and for the bigger picture that I couldn't even quite see yet. I had learned how showing up in those moments would lead me somewhere—to a summit, a gorgeous view, the feeling of gratitude . . . and satisfaction in myself for not quitting or giving up. Those brick-by-brick, step-by-step moments gave me energy and purpose to continue to show up throughout my recovery.

4 SURVIVAL

The day I retired my scooter and casts was terrifying. Yes, I was thrilled that my body was healing, but as I took my first steps down the street—Pearl Street, to be exact, a pedestrian mall in Boulder, Colorado—I felt naked. I was without my boot or arm casts, without the safety net of my scooter, without something that screamed, "Steer clear of me! I'm injured." I was terrified.

Heading to my favorite coffee shop, Spruce Confections, like I had almost every day for the past few months, I clung to the sides of buildings as I walked, terrified I might get trampled. I wanted more space. I wondered why people weren't being more careful around me. Didn't they know what had happened to me? I was just learning to walk. Couldn't they see I was scared and limping? I had passed by these shops and places yesterday on my scooter and been granted looks of sympathy and extra maneuvering room. Didn't they recognize me? Didn't they know these were my first unassisted steps in months?

As I looked into the faces of these people, who just yesterday were stopping, helping me, opening doors, or moving around me to give me more space, there was no recognition. No acknowledgment. I seemed normal to them. I looked "normal." No one had *any* idea what I had just been through. What I was still going through as I struggled to find my stride and learn to walk again. The world felt new and foreign to me. The harshness of the concrete underfoot was no comfort to my foot, and the sympathetic nature and kind actions I had witnessed from these strangers had turned fickle.

But in that moment, after my initial frustration and disbelief, I had an epiphany. *I have no idea what everyone* else *has been through to get to right here, right now in front of me.* I had no idea what these people were going through in that exact moment as they walked down the street, just as I was. I looked at faces as they passed by. *What is she thinking? Is he going through a hardship?* I started to wonder about the stories behind the faces I passed. I dreamed up tales of struggle and happiness, loss and strength, as I read the expressions on each one. It was in that moment I realized we were all connected by the silent struggles and battles of life. They were all fighting something too, just as I was. They were all in the process of overcoming and finding their way. Just as I was. We were all fighting. Surviving.

I had crossed the threshold into the true battle for survival. In the next few months I had to relearn how to walk, how to live, how to set new goals and thrive again. I remember those first steps vividly. How apprehensive I felt, afraid, hesitant, wondering if my body would remember what to do.

I was overwhelmed by how much work I still had to do. My body didn't feel like my own, and I wasn't sure how to interact with it. We were learning together again, and I didn't feel like me. How was I supposed to get myself back?

I read a lot of books, searching for meaning and keeping my mind occupied so I wouldn't feel compelled to push my body too hard physically. One of my favorites was *Deep Survival* by

Laurence Gonzales. It was recommended to me because it discusses the nature of accidents in the mountains and recounts the stories of those who survived. But even with the relevance to my own story, as I read the back cover, I knew I wanted to read this book for the "why."

This whole time I had been wondering why I had survived my accident. Did I have something in common with the people in his book? Was there an explanation for me? I had to find out.

It was a thought-provoking read. I was amazed by the horrific experiences people had gone through and come out alive. I felt a kinship with these people, like we had seen something, or experienced something, together—even though their stories seemed more horrific and intense than my own.

The book explores the reasons why people survive horrific accidents, by recounting what happened to them and how they reacted, the plan they made, and how they executed that plan. It talks about basic survival techniques, such as attending classes and getting training or various certifications, from beginner pins to expert badges, to deem an individual "mountain ready."

What struck me was that the majority of those who attended these wilderness classes and got certifications were the ones who were the most inept and ill-equipped to deal with a real-life survival situation. Of course, this is not a justification or argument to skip wilderness-preparedness classes, but it is an acknowledgment that there is more to survival than what you learn in a classroom or from others. A huge part of surviving or adapting to an unfamiliar situation comes from being present in the moment, staying observant, and reacting to your surroundings calmly and deliberately.

Something that stood out to me in Gonzales's writing and storytelling was how these people were faced with the same choice, every single one of them. And when tested, they actively chose the same thing: to keep living, even in dire circumstances. No amount of survival training could have taught them that. Sure, they all knew some basic survival skills, but in the moment when they were tested and couldn't rely on anything other than themselves and their own intuition, they chose to not give up. They found a way to survive.

I'm talking about survival in the moment of an accident, and the inevitable problem-solving that was necessary to come out on the other side. Each story in Gonzales's book was very different, but the persistence to live and the refusal to give up was a common thread. Faced with any problem or impossible obstacle—lack of food, shelter, or water; new injuries; or wavering hope—these people found a solution to keep moving. Their will to survive was stronger.

I couldn't help but wonder what allowed me to survive my fall and accident. Sure, I wasn't alone. I had help and a helicopter rescue. It wasn't like I needed to hike my broken body back to civilization. But I wondered how or why I didn't sustain more serious injuries. After reading a chapter in Gonzales's book describing the story of a man who had taken a bad fall off a mountain while climbing, I found myself reliving my own fall. He described how the world slowed down, that he remembered the impacts and observed the fact that he was falling—the same thing that happened to me.

He remembered relaxing, letting the fall happen. It was acceptance that this might, in fact, be the end. That he might die. There wasn't anything he could do about it but fall, relax, and figure out a way to get through when it was over. I had the same thought process when I was falling. I, too, accepted my demise and calmly observed as I felt each successive impact on the mountainside until I came to a stop. It was a logical, peaceful acceptance—not that I was giving up or wanted to die, but that it was out of my control at the moment, so I had to just let it happen.

I believe this acceptance caused me to relax while I fell, instead of being rigid and stiff with fear, which might have caused more serious injuries. My body somehow found a way to survive as I was falling down that mountainside. Subconsciously, I seemed to know exactly what to do to protect myself and keep living. This was the first step to survival: acceptance. Not passive acceptance of death, or welcoming it, but a resilient acceptance, knowing this may kill me, but still fighting like hell when I had the chance.

I value integrity. It's one of the core values I hold most dear, in both myself and those I choose to spend time with. Integrity, to me, means being authentic and honest, no matter who is looking or paying attention to you. It's a quality that's dying, especially in a world in which attention and "likes" and self-indulgence and narcissism are rewarded.

When I'm outside, nothing else matters. Not the current trends or what I'm wearing or the latest gossip . . . nothing matters but the here and now. The outdoors, especially the mountains, are the best example of living in the moment, with integrity. They don't apologize for what they are. They are beautiful, majestic, gritty, dangerous, fickle, and incredibly intricate. They are constantly changing, different each time you wander into them. They don't apologize for it; it's who they are. They require respect, demand it. And it doesn't matter what route I have planned that day. If their capricious nature decides to bring in a storm, that's how it will be. I'd better be ready for it or be ready to change my plans. The mountains and Mother Nature make the rules—and I'm sometimes lucky enough to get to play once in a while.

This powerful presence is what I love most about the mountains. Their brutal honesty teaches me to be the best version of myself. When I'm out there, I have to be extremely present in the moment, and aware that the line between light and dark is one and the same.

I must tread lightly, respecting their power and my smallness, my insignificance. Every time I enter into an adventure in the mountains, I accept and understand there is a certain risk involved—always. It's on my most routine runs I must especially acknowledge the risk of my endeavor. It's a tricky balance. When something is familiar, it's easy to think that there is less danger, but that's not true. Going on a trail by yourself from your own front door, with no food and water or even a cell phone to contact someone, and not telling anyone your route because you might not know it yourself and you want to see how you feel, is wonderful. It's what I love to do. But is it smart? Is it safe? Is it risk-free simply because I've done it so many times and nothing has happened before?

That's a common justification that I, and many others, use when training in the mountains. But after my accident and reading about or discussing other mountain accidents, many of which happened on familiar terrain—a rock stepped on a million times, or a route known from memory—I know for certain that familiarity doesn't ensure safety, or eliminate risk. It just creates that illusion. No matter the route or degree of familiarity, there is still a certain risk involved when you enter a mountain playground. That risk might approach zero, but it never actually gets there.

The mountains are a perfect example of the fragility of life. Contained in their beauty is both life and death, darkness and brightness. You can't have one without the other, and to think that the mountains are only made for happy memories and good training sessions is both naïve and narrow-minded.

I've understood this from the outset of my running career. It's a result of growing up in the mountains, spending copious amounts of time observing them, camping surrounded by them, and exploring their changing features. There is a subtle fear, a respect, knowing they make the rules. But that doesn't stop me from enjoying their beauty—it adds to it.

I know I must take certain risks in order to do what I love. Even though my accident changed my life and nearly killed me,

I KNOW I MUST TAKE CERTAIN RISKS IN ORDER TO DO WHAT I LOVE. EVEN THOUGH MY ACCIDENT CHANGED MY LIFE AND NEARLY KILLED ME, I UNDERSTOOD AND ACCEPTED THAT THESE THINGS CAN HAPPEN.

I understood and accepted that these things can happen. I had accepted this fact before my accident, and I also had to accept it after the accident. I couldn't stay angry; I couldn't be afraid to go back to what I loved. The fickle nature and danger of the mountains, the risk they contain, is constant. They are constant in their fickleness. It's part of their integrity. I couldn't blame them for it or spend my life avoiding their nature. Instead, it was my responsibility to relearn my mountain skills so I could regain my confidence to enter into them again, and to accept the risk involved in doing what I love.

The mountains have also taught me patience. The double facets of the mountains—the light and darkness—mirror the emotions and experiences of life. Life is not always bright and happy. It can be really hard, but that doesn't mean it is any less beautiful or meaningful. In fact, I think these experiences add to the beauty of life. Some of the most beautiful moments I've experienced in the mountains involve constantly shifting clouds, moving in and out across the horizon, fog obscuring the way—or misty sunrises.

The constant changes I witness in the mountains make them enjoyable. Of course, a bluebird day in the mountains is wonderful and beautiful, but it can also be boring in its consistent, predictable beauty. Mountains—like life—contain variation and disparity. The bitterness of defeat only makes the victorious moments more joyous. The misery brought on by suffering brings more genuine contentment in the times when life is enjoyable, stress-free, and easy. Times of melancholy allow room for appreciation when life makes sense and you feel happy for no reason at all.

There is room for all of these emotions in life; they add to one another. The mountains are what showed me this. In tandem with their power, death and destruction, avalanches, fires, and brutal storms, they offer beautiful sunrises and sunsets, meadows filled with wildflowers, lakes, flowing streams, fresh strawberries, and wild landscapes that seem endless with possibility. Both sides are necessary—to truly experience happiness, you must experience pain.

Each person in *Deep Survival* faced extreme suffering. They also accepted it as an inevitable part of their survival story. Each person discovered new light and learning as a result—not new survival techniques, like how to build a shelter or make a fire or hunt for squirrels. These survivors experienced a huge learning curve in adjusting to life after their accident and feat of survival.

Many of the people in Gonzales's book shared how it wasn't hard surviving in the moment—that was the easy part. It was surviving after the fact, in regular life—learning how to be themselves again, feeling different and changed. That was hard. That was their real struggle for survival.

I felt the exact same way. Day one of survival for me was *not* the day I lay on the mountainside by my friends, waiting for the mountain rescue team. It wasn't when those mountain rescue men hoisted me onto the helicopter and took me to the hospital. Survival didn't start for me when the team of doctors in Norway cleaned me up, set my bones, and left me sleeping in the care of the wonderful nursing staff who monitored me for weeks. Survival didn't start when I came home and had more surgeries to repair my still-broken body. Survival didn't even begin when I was learning to move around in the world as an injured person who couldn't walk, carry anything, or care for herself.

My survival began the day those casts came off and I was asked to start walking again, to start living again. Outwardly I looked "normal," but I wasn't the same. I didn't feel the same. I was changed, different. Everything was new around me, and I was truly in "survival mode." Once again, I had to find my way in this world.

This was the hardest part of the journey. This was the time when I had to fight for every step and slowly get back to what my body could do. Even after all the physical and emotional trauma I had endured, I was faced with a choice. Do I give up? Or do I fight? I had to choose to fight, to survive and keep going in my post-survival state. Even when I wanted to give up or didn't see the point, something inside wouldn't let me.

I was reminded of the purpose of my suffering or hopelessness every time I looked to the mountains. They, too, were changing, constantly evolving in their brutal, unforgiving way. And I still found them beautiful in their fickle rawness. So, I had to keep going too. I had to be ugly and upset and sad; those feelings helped me problem-solve. I learned not only to find a way to keep going but also how to discover my new self and the happiness it would eventually bring. I learned to accept my difficult reality while remaining persistent and hopeful that I would survive this phase in my life.

The stories I read in *Deep Survival* wove tales of people surviving against all odds and going back to their "normal" lives wiser and full of life. I had that opportunity too. I had survived, and I was learning to survive again. I was uncovering and rediscovering aspects of myself that I thought were only useful for pushing myself to achieve my athletic goals. I was changing, and letting those experiences change me, and adapting. That's what survival is about anyway—observing your surroundings and being ready to react, change, and find new solutions to life's problems.

Survival was no longer scary. Just because it was unfamiliar territory and I was unpracticed at learning to function in a world I thought I might not be a part of, this wasn't a reason to retreat into a dimmer or different version of myself. It was a time for learning and reflection. A time to search for the reasons to live and be a part of this world and bring to it what I knew, what I was learning, and what I am still learning now.

It was a time to be honest. To have integrity, even when I felt like a mess and didn't know which way was up or what I wanted out of life anymore. This aspect of survival and rediscovery of self was where the real work was, and continues to be. There is no easy class to take or certification to earn, no level of readiness that can be achieved. This aspect of life is unpredictable and uncomfortable, yet necessary. We aren't automatically ready when tough things happen to us. They usually catch us by surprise and seem like an unwelcomed burden or obstacle. But we are instinctively prepared. If we are willing to welcome the discomfort that comes with growth and change, we can begin to shift our perspective and learn from those experiences.

Everything that has happened to us, good or bad, shapes our perspectives and forms our views. Our experiences influence how we behave, how we react, and how we emotionally cope. We are habitual creatures, reacting to the stimuli we have in front of us, and sometimes we're puzzled or frozen in the face of new stimuli or situations. But we do have the skills to overcome new challenges, even if they are unfamiliar and foreign. How? We simply *try*.

Let go of expectation, and you learn as you go. You learn from your mistakes and often you learn the hard way, through failure—time and time again. But through each failure you learn something new to bring to the next situation, and you learn from that one too. Maybe you fail again, but you're not deprived of a lesson. After failure, you may be ready to approach the situation from a new angle with new aptitude.

Never in my life had I sustained so many injuries or been asked to adapt so much and endure such a recovery. But instead of becoming tense with avoidance, fear, and reluctance, I calmly (and sometimes not so calmly) accepted my reality and fought like hell when I had the chance. This was my survival. Physical and emotional. I was living it bravely and unapologetically, doing the best I could, learning from each situation. Failing, but getting up to try again the next day. Refusing to give up.

This is real survival. It's not clear-cut, and it's not contained to one instant. Survival is ongoing, and every one of us contributes to our survival on a daily basis. It's a recurrent practice, and it's never really over. But this is what adds to the magnificence of life—the constant change and appreciation you gain from each peak or valley. You can't have one without the other.

Whenever my hope wavers or fades, I look to the mountains for guidance and conviction. I remember that they, too, are constantly changing; that's what I love most about them. Their seasons are short and sweet, causing me to relish every second of each one while it lasts.

So it is with the brutal winter, its frigid air and cold, crisp mornings. Bundling up in the dark before skinning up the mountainside to meet the late sunrise and enjoy the shorter days. Knowing that, soon enough, the snow will melt into a wet spring, full of warm thunderstorms, luscious green hills filled with wildflowers. Still, there will also be that surprise spring snowfall, heavy and wet. I must enjoy those cool mornings as the days grow longer and hotter, bringing summer into full swing, with sweltering dry heat and opportunities to explore ridgelines and mountaintops by foot. Now I can go out on all-day adventures, because the sun refuses to set until 10 p.m. Even as I watch the late-night sunset, I know that this season, too, is fleeting. The days will grow short again as the glow of golden aspen leaves sparkling and rustling in the wind welcomes the coming of winter.

All of this change is beautiful. I love each season, and my appreciation for each is reinforced by their fleeting nature. If I can love the mountains for their unpredictable beauty, it's only fitting to welcome those aspects in my personal life and learn to grow and change in the seasons of life. To understand and accept their impermanence, knowing that I will survive and become wiser because of it.

THE POWER OF BELIEF 5

Despite the challenges of my injuries, I am certain that my best physical and mental days are ahead—that being the best athlete I can ever be is only possible because of the challenges I face now. Believe.

S ometimes I think the mind is the strongest part of an athlete. It's not the legs or lungs or heart, but the mind. Strength comes from how an athlete handles pressure and pain and problem-solves when things go south.

I wrote this mantra down two weeks after I was told I would never run again: *Believe. Believe your best athletic days are ahead of you. Believe in your power, believe in your strength, don't stop believing.* Some days I looked at these words and shook my head. How could believing make any difference? Believing doesn't do my training for me, or get me up a mountain on a hot summer day. My legs do that, my strength does that, my body does that. I needed to be strong physically. Believing, I thought, had no part in getting me there.

But the more I thought about it, the more I realized how much power belief holds. I've realized that it's what keeps me going, what keeps me curious.

Believing that I can run far is what allows me to try.

Believing forces me to do a hard workout, a new trail, a new race, a new challenge.

Believing is what separates me from those who never try, or those who give up when it gets too hard.

Believing is a challenge, but faith in myself and how I will benefit or grow through the process is a strength more powerful than any muscle or lung.

Believing is what gets me up mountains and through tough races. If I *believe* in the power of my legs, they take me farther and faster than I ever thought possible. It's like giving yourself permission to fly, or to dream. If you eliminate the limits, the possibilities are endless. And it all starts with belief.

When everyone said I couldn't do it, that I'd never run another step, I was devastated. But only for a few minutes. No, just kidding; this sadness lasted several months, arriving in various waves of intensity. There were many moments after my accident when running again felt nearly impossible, but I wanted to believe that maybe one day I would. Belief is what sparked the journey.

Belief also taught me about the power of community and the impact others can have on you—what it means to put out love, connection, and community to the world. I live in Boulder, Colorado, which has a reputation as a hippie town. You might roll your eyes at the "Send love out into the world and you will receive" kind of mantra—it sounds pretty stereotypically Boulder and oh so "granola"—but this mentality had an impact on me.

The more vulnerable I became in my injured state, asking for and receiving help, the more help I was able to give in return.

Although it didn't happen instantly, once I was healthier, I realized that on the long road of recovery I had formed a community of wonderful people who were giving and caring.

My community selflessly took care of me when I needed it—from my physical therapist, who kept the gym open late, listened to me cry, and told me it was all going to be OK, to my mother, who watched me struggle and supported me in the process of starting to run again.

My mother was scared for me to run again. She knew that I didn't just want to run. I wanted to race and even return to skyrunning—the very thing that nearly killed me. But she set aside her own fears and supported me through the process. That support allowed me to be there for her when she was faced with breast cancer. As she voiced her fears, her frustrations, and her gratitude for being alive, I was better equipped to help her from my own experience in recovery.

Another important person in my community was my friend Liz Saenz, who was there for me on my bad days. She was going through her own injury recovery and dealing with her own demons about getting back to mountain bike racing after a bad crash and subsequent surgeries. We developed a type of buddy system. We texted every morning, making plans about car pickups and drop-offs. In those check-ins, we were able to confide in each other. I'd tell her if I was feeling unmotivated and didn't want to go to physical therapy. Liz would text back, "Me neither, girlfriend, but we gotta keep showing up. We're in this together."

Sometimes on those mornings, we'd cry in the car together before making it into PT. We didn't need to say much; just having the permission and space to be sad next to each other was enough. It was real, raw. Since I couldn't drive and Liz had to come get me, it forced her to keep showing up too. We also had happy dates: coffee dates, to be precise. Giggling and laughing over the silliest things. We'd sometimes get the whole coffee shop looking over at us as we laughed so hard we started crying. We were a team with an unspoken bond. It brought us closer and made us stronger—together.

This give-and-take was one of the most powerful experiences I carried with me throughout my recovery and return to running and daily life. In challenging times, I remembered to put out good energy and ask for help, knowing that when I had the strength, I could do that in turn for someone else.

Learning to run again was a scary process. It wasn't straightforward. There was a lot of fear around my foot injury. Ligaments are tricky. Because of their restricted blood flow, they take a very long time to heal. Some studies have shown that full ligament repair (depending on the location) can take up to two years. Logically, I knew this. So, when I was cleared to start walking after two and a half months of no weight-bearing, I knew my foot was not going to feel great.

That day I was in the doctor's office for a checkup. I was meeting with the physician's assistant, Alan, who had helped Dr. Gorman perform the surgery. He took off my boot and examined the incision and the new X-rays. After taking a look and doing some routine mobility tests on my foot and ankle, he turned to me and said, "Well, it's time to start walking."

My eyes grew wide as I took a big gulp to clear my throat. "Wait, what?" This wasn't what I was expecting. "I can start walking? When?"

Alan turned to my mother, rolling my scooter toward her. "You can take this." He turned back to me and said, "Now! Let's take a few practice steps." He gave me the walking boot to put back on and instructed me to start walking around the office. I was apprehensive at first, limping, half-weighting my foot, and not taking full strides. Alan encouraged me, telling me it would take time; I'd get used to it. I also needed to get a bigger shoe for my left foot, one with a higher sole to match the height of my boot, which was now a walking boot. A new challenge started now.

Those first few steps hurt. A lot. I knew muscle atrophy happens quickly, but it was hard to believe the change. My calf, once ridiculously strong, was skinny and appeared to be deteriorating right before my eyes. I had noticed this before, but now that I was walking, I was astonished by its lack of function and how quickly my body had adapted to not moving. My calf got sore from just those first ten steps in the doctor's office! The pain in my foot was intense. It was like I was stepping on needles, even when I wasn't walking. Alan assured me this was normal. "The nerves will grow back. They are just extra sensitive right now," he said.

My mom's eyes filled with tears as she watched me struggle. She knew it was the beginning of a long journey. We made another appointment to come back in four weeks. I reached for my scooter out of reflex, blushing as I realized I didn't need it anymore. As Alan opened the door and I attempted to walk down the corridor of the doctor's office, I felt two things: pain—with each step—and apprehension. I didn't know how to move my body anymore. Slowly, I made my way to the elevator and out the front door to the parking lot.

"I'm at the beginning again," I said to my mother as she pulled out of the parking lot.

"You'll be OK, Hillary, just take it one day at a time. This is a huge step forward."

I felt wobbly and unstable for weeks. Those first four weeks in the boot, learning to walk again, were painful. I had never experienced nerve damage, but apparently, there are a lot of nerves on the bottom of your foot. Have you heard of the homunculus? It's a depiction of the ratio of nerves associated with each region of our body. It equates the size of the body part with the number of sensory neurons in them. So, on a human, the lips are HUGE, along with the tongue, the hands, the face, another body part I won't mention here, and, of course, the feet.

To my surprise, many of these numerous neurons in my foot had died in the two and a half months I hadn't been walking. After my mom dropped me off from the doctor's office at my apartment, I decided to try walking again—for real this time. Around my neighborhood. Thankfully the sidewalks were dry, so I went inside, grabbed my jacket, and headed out the door. Even those first few steps to my front door felt like a million tiny pins pricking me with each step. Those pins bounced around my foot as I pressed down and rolled through my foot strike. I tried my best to not favor one side of my foot and land as normally as possible with each step. But I was clearly favoring the outside of my right foot, avoiding pressing through my big toe and arch, where Dr. Gorman had operated on the injured ligament.

I immediately became anxious, frustrated, and scared. My mind started racing, drawing conclusions and drastic worst-case scenarios: *What If I develop a permanent limp? Or an altered gait? I can't have that for running; it will lead to injury.* As I made my way back to my front door, I carried those concerns and doubts with me. It had only been my first day back to walking and instead of celebrating my ability to go up and down stairs successfully, I immediately started worrying. I didn't want to keep walking. Fear had crept back in.

Even when I wasn't walking, or had only walked for ten minutes, those nerves were overactive, sending pain signals to my brain. They even fired when I was sleeping, causing phantom pain, a burning sensation along with a dull ache and a feeling of restlessness. Those overactive nerves were like my thoughts.

Eventually, the fear subsided, along with the pain. Those nerves grew back and started firing appropriately, and the pain became more infrequent and predictable.

But the limp didn't go away.

I had developed a psychogenic limp—something I never would have expected. Logically, it didn't make sense—my foot was getting back to normal—but subconsciously, which we know very little about in the first place, I was still hurting.

My body was protecting me from something. My body knew that I was injured, and it had developed a pattern to protect me. Hence the limp and favoring one side. I was still in physical therapy, working to regain normal function and range in my body, but I didn't know what to do to work past this.

Thanks to my new community and my willingness to be vulnerable, people from all over the world reached out to help me. After receiving an Instagram message from this guy who specializes in injury recovery based on manual and physiological manipulation, I decided to give it a try, although I was skeptical.

Levi Younger met with me over tea (I'm more of a coffee drinker, strike one) in Boulder to discuss his method: Rolfing. This is a type of alternative medicine similar to deep-tissue massage, but with a focus on the whole body (and mind). I wasn't convinced. What I had heard about Rolfing was the more painful the manual manipulation, the better. And I was already in a lot of pain.

But when Levi started to talk about the psychological effects of pain, and how those effects can create permanent neural pathways or habits, forcing us to form imbalances in our physical bodies, I started to listen. My neuroscience brain perked up, and I began drawing parallels to what I had learned in graduate school about neuroplasticity and the brain's ability to go into "survival mode," like post-traumatic stress disorder (PTSD).

Levi explained that I had experienced a traumatic event, and my body had rewired my neural circuitry to protect me in the future. It had learned my foot was injured when I wasn't using it, and the limp was a way to protect me from hurting it again. I needed my body and brain to learn that it wasn't hurt anymore. I knew I was healing, but my brain didn't know that yet. That's when I started working with Levi on the physical aspect of my recovery—breaking up scar tissues and working on mobility—and also the psychological aspect.

The process was like cultivating belief in my body again. I needed a safe space to explore the movements of my body and, in particular, my injured foot. Levi had me do simple exercises, like placing a block up against the arch of my right foot while I rocked my weight back and forth onto it or went into a single-leg squat. At first, I thought this was silly, and that these small adjustments wouldn't do anything. Was I just wasting my time? Crying, I would become frustrated and filled with negativity at the slow process. But Levi kept reminding me to be patient, to be kind to my body, and to give it time to heal.

One afternoon, three weeks in, I was rocking back and forth on that block, counting to ten as I prepared to walk around the room. My mind was somewhere else, discouraged by the slow progress and the lack of feeling I had in my own body. Was I ever going to feel my foot normally again?

Levi touched my foot. "Find your big toe," he said.

I rolled my eyes and said under my breath, "I can see my big toe. It's right there."

Levi laughed and looked up at me. "Feeling a bit feisty today are we, Hillary?"

I smiled and gave him a more honest answer. "It hurts when I push through my big toe."

Levi had me do ten more rocks back and forth on the block and said, "OK, now let's have you walk around." I started to walk, thinking to myself, *This is stupid . . . how could this help?* Levi could sense the doubts floating around in my head. "How does it feel?" he asked.

As I focused back into my body and onto my foot, my thoughts and doubts began to soften. I began to focus on the feeling, finding my big toe and rolling through my gait. I realized something felt different this time, sturdier. The limp was less pronounced. In that moment, all the mindless, simple, stupid exercises suddenly meant something: hope. I began to feel hope.

That shred of hope and belief began to grow, and I began to understand more about the power of my mind and my attitude and how those both affected the pain and fear surrounding my injuries. I was able to push past my injury and believe again in my body's capabilities. The trick was simply believing—and, in turn, reforming my perception around fear and what I thought my body was capable of.

This new belief system made me hyperaware of my surroundings. Suddenly, I was aware of every step. Some days I felt fear kicking in or negative emotions welling up, but instead of letting those feelings influence my actions (catastrophizing my injuries, favoring my injured foot, and ultimately walking with a limp), I consciously acknowledged my fear, told myself it was OK to be afraid, reminded myself to be patient, and repeated a positive affirmation to cultivate a positive perspective.

Believe that your best athletic days are ahead of you.

You are more than a result.

You are enough, just as you are.

Once I repeated the affirmations enough—some days I had to repeat this process multiple times—the negative thoughts had no room anymore, leaving me to focus on what I *could* do, on what my body was adapting to and healing from. It was an essential process for me to choose to believe in myself, rather than let fear, expectation, and doubt get the best of me. It's what led me to come back from my injuries without feeling the pressure of a comeback. Letting go of expectation allowed me to celebrate even the smallest victories, to be utterly in the winning moment and thankful for my current state.

Of course, I'm not perfect. I was frustrated by the pain, the slow progress. And I dreamed of competing and running freely. I still believed that I could and would run again, but that belief had room to breathe. Though I wanted it, badly and wholeheartedly, I knew I didn't need it.

I didn't need to compete again to be happy. I didn't need that to feel whole or complete. I knew I was enough just as I was. I believed I was enough without that part of me. Even though running had always made my life feel brighter, happier, and healthier, there's a difference between *needing* it and *wanting* it. Recognizing that separation ignited a fire within me to understand the power of my will and construct a path to attain what I wanted: to run.

Right around the time I was cleared to walk, my coach introduced me to another one of his athletes, Lizi Bolanos-Nauth. Lizi had torn her tensor fasciae latae ligament and was also starting the process of running again. We teamed up and tackled the process together.

On our first outing together, we couldn't run yet but we could hike, so we decided to climb our local mountain, Mount Sanitas, and do some steep hiking laps. This trail climbs 1,300 feet in about a mile and a half. It's a great low-impact workout.

On a cold January day, Lizi and I met at 5:30 a.m. to do some laps on the mountain. Since we couldn't run, we planned to hike up as fast as we could and then gingerly hike back down and repeat. We strapped on our headlamps in the dark. Lizi had never run with a headlamp before, but that didn't matter. We were in it together. My confidence gave her confidence. I took the lead as we headed up the frosty trail single file, every exhalation a white wisp before our faces, illuminated by our headlamps. The uphill part of the trail was steep and included a mix of stairs and big rocks you had to boost yourself over. I liked this type of "running"—we call it "power hiking" in the ultra-world—since hiking fast uphill is actually faster than running uphill. Lizi, who's about a foot shorter than me, had her legs near her head as she moved over some of the larger rocks on the trail.

We were both tentative on the downhill section, carefully

placing our footsteps on solid ground and moving deliberately around the rocks as we talked our way through it. The sun started to come up, and we stashed our headlamps as we gained confidence and speed on the downhill. That morning we did three laps.

From that first meetup on a dark, frigid January morning, Lizi and I never ran out of things to talk about. It was the start of a beautiful friendship. We could share with each other the struggles of the process—sometimes in silence and other times in full anguish of our frustrations—how hard it felt that day, or how impatient we were with recovery. Through it all, we were patient with one another, allowing the frustrations to have their place while at the same time keeping each other from getting too discouraged. Lizi and I tackled a lot of firsts together.

Colorado winters aren't straightforward. One day might be completely sunny, a cool 50 degrees, then the next day the skies dump snow and the trails turn to ice. But Lizi and I didn't let that hold us back. Instead of staying inside, we each bought a pair of microspikes and strapped them on for snowy, icy morning hikes. We wanted to be safe, but we also knew we needed to feed our souls and not feel trapped in our bodies or by our injuries. Having each other there for support certainly made the process easier.

Lizi's return to running was faster than mine. Our coach had prescribed her run-walk-run-walk intervals to get back to a running stride, but I was hesitant and scared to try running. My foot still ached all the time while hiking, especially on the downhill. I knew it was "healing" pain, but I didn't want to aggravate the healing process by running. Plus, I just didn't know if I could do it. My body was still fearful of that movement.

Later that month I had another appointment with the doctors. Alan had given me the go-ahead to start walking at my last appointment, but this time I was meeting with Dr. Gorman. The last time I had seen her, she told me that I would never compete again, that I would never run again. Those words were in my brain as I sat in the exam room with her, waiting to hear what she would say next.

When she told me I could try "jogging," I couldn't believe my ears. Was I hearing her right? Was I really OK to try this? I looked at Dr. Gorman in disbelief. She met my eyes and said, "Yes, you can jog. It's going to be a long process still. Your arch was severely injured. That's a foot-changing injury. You might never run at the same level as before, but you have to start somewhere."

Jog. I hate that word. It feels like an insult to the movement of running. A consolation prize. A compromise. I wasn't going to *jog*—I was going to run.

When I left my appointment with Dr. Gorman, I drove straight to a trailhead instead of home. This uphill trail was more like a gravel road. It didn't have rocks, roots, or technical sections of any kind. Just a wide-open trail. That eased my mind a bit, but still, I was nervous. It was a cold day. The trees were frosted white, and snow was sprinkled along the sides of the path. I scanned the ground for any sign of ice or precipitation that might make me lose my balance.

As I began hiking up the trail, I could see my breath in the air in front of me. I started to move more deliberately, increasing my pace, but I was still hesitant and doubted if my body knew what to do. Could I still run? I wasn't sure it knew how anymore. After about ten minutes of hiking, I quickened my pace and my stride. I finally took one foot off the ground as the other planted, and I started to run.

Each step on my injured foot was painful and awkward. Everything was new again, like learning how to walk and move my body. I wasn't used to the impact. My body would recoil a bit, and I would limp and grimace in anticipation of landing on my injured foot. I continued to run for about thirty seconds, letting my body feel the once-familiar motions. Once I stopped and slowed to transition to a hike, a huge smile broke across my face. My eyes were wide and full. "I just ran!"

I walked for another couple minutes, and then started to run again. This time the motion came a bit more fluidly. I ran for a full minute. As I slowed to a walk again, excitement coursed through me. I wanted to jump up and down and dance around the trail! The running motion was feeling less awkward. I was ecstatic and smiling nonstop! But thoughts of that Norwegian mountainside crept in. Along with feeling exhilarated, I was simultaneously fearful and tense. I picked up my stride, relishing in the pitter-patter noise of my feet up the trail and the crunch of the shifting gravel beneath my feet. I caught myself whispering aloud between steps, "Don't fall, don't fall, don't fall." I was still scared. My body knew that the last time I had done this motion, I nearly died. I let myself repeat those words—"Don't fall, don't fall, don't fall"—in unison with my right foot striking the ground. I was embracing emotions of both excitement and caution.

I repeated this cycle—one minute on, one minute off, one minute on, one minute off—until I reached the top of the hill, 1.5 miles from where I started. I felt so proud, happy, and hopeful. I declared to myself again, louder this time, "I JUST RAN!"

Running definitely didn't feel normal yet, and I knew I had a long way to go, but I couldn't contain my excitement. I immediately called my coach. I was practically yelling when I told him the news.

"Good job, Goat!" Adam said. "Congratulations on starting the process. I'm so proud of you." I hung up the phone, eager to start regaining my confidence—and to start running again.

I was ecstatic about my progress and my return to running. That evening, and in the following days, my foot began aching from the new motion, but I called my physical therapist and we discussed it as "normal, healing pain." It was safe to proceed. It wasn't comfortable or straightforward, but it didn't have to be. I kept believing it was possible, and that faith kept me pushing through the pain and discomfort. I continued working with Levi, addressing the pain that accompanied motion. I still believed I could work through this.

Even with the joy of being able to run again coursing through me, I didn't attempt another run until a week later. Lizi was traveling with her family, and while she was away she had started her first run-walk progressions as well. I thought our early-morning hiking adventures might be over, that her recovery was taking off and I was stuck in mine.

When she came home, she invited me to run-walk with her. I was nervous. Would she be too fast for me? Would my foot hurt too much? Would I be too scared to try running again? How would my foot feel? Focused on cultivating my positive beliefs and the joy that brought me, I pushed the negative thoughts and anxious emotions to the side. Lizi and I were in this together and we believed, together, that we would both run again.

Those first morning runs were on completely flat ground. Both trail runners, we craved the up-and-down and the variability of mountain terrain—the uphill, in particular. We chose a flat path that overlooked the Indian Peaks Wilderness and the Boulder Skyline. This route gave us perspective in our preparation before we could get back to the terrain we loved. Plus, since it was still January, we endured some pretty intense weather, with cold temperatures, ice, and wind—so we were thankful, short-term, not to be on the trails yet.

But soon our time came. Later that month we were ready to combine running with our beloved steep trails, where it was necessary to hike briskly (power hike) to the top, before "jogging" down.

We did this on our familiar local trail, Mount Sanitas, which was the shortest peak of the Boulder Skyline but boasted steep terrain. This trail, lower in elevation, remained fairly clear during the inevitable weather fronts expected over the weekend. Plus, with constant foot traffic, it was our safest bet to be reunited with our trails.

For our first Mount Sanitas run-walk, hiking up and slowly running down was the plan. Those nervous feelings flooded through me again. What if Lizi was too fast for me? She was further along in her recovery than I was, and I hadn't been running that much. My stomach turned in nervous anticipation, and I took several deep breaths before meeting her on the trail. *Believe you can do this. You can do this.* As we started out, hiking at first on the uphill section, we started talking and laughing like normal. "I'm so glad you are here," Lizi said to me. "It gives me confidence to do this with someone."

I smiled. "We're in this together."

In less than an hour we had finished the round trip, about 3.5 miles, and half of that was running. We were both smiling ear to ear when we finished, consumed with joy in our accomplishments. "Thank you!" Lizi said as she gave me a big hug. "Now, when are we doing this again?"

But our coach didn't let us get too comfortable. Before long, Adam had prescribed us Mount Sanitas repeats. We started at two repeats—up and down the mountain once, then repeat. But as the weeks progressed, we worked up to three repeats, and then four!

By February, six months post-operation, I was up to about 14 miles, half of them running. We were progressing. We were getting better. More and more I believed that running, and running long distances, was possible again.

But I was at a crossroads. In the surgery to repair the ligament in my foot, two screws were placed to bridge the gap where the ligament had broken. Those screws were holding me together; they were keeping my foot in place and encouraging the healing of the ligament. But we couldn't know for sure how the ligament was progressing. An X-ray wouldn't show the ligament, and we couldn't do an MRI because of the screws in my foot.

The only way to test my progress was to keep running and

I WAS HAPPY BUT COMPLETELY TERRIFIED. HOW WOULD I STACK UP? IT WASN'T A RACE—I KNEW THAT—BUT THAT COMPETITIVE SIDE IS HARD TO TURN OFF, AND WHEN THAT GUN RANG OUT IN THE CRISP AIR, MY ANXIOUS RACE NERVES KICKED INTO ADRENALINE.

continue to do the strength work and jumping progressions my physical therapist had prescribed. He monitored my progress and assured me, as best he could, that my foot was indeed healing.

But in February, about five weeks after I was cleared to start "jogging" by Dr. Gorman, I went in for a checkup and an X-ray. The X-ray revealed that one of the screws in my foot had broken. We needed to schedule a surgery to remove them.

This wasn't unexpected. A metal paper clip is strong, but if you bend it enough, it will eventually break. That's exactly what happened to the screw in my foot. My surgery was scheduled for Valentine's Day. Fitting, really. I had developed a relationship with the screws in my foot. I had relied on them, been hard on them, grown to love them, but I was ready to move on. Before parting ways and enduring another surgery, I scheduled a trip to Utah to participate in a Running Up For Air (RUFA) event outside of Salt Lake City on Grandeur Peak. I wanted one last hurrah with my screws before I had surgery—and another recovery.

This event was a special one. It combined running, fundraising, and scientific awareness of air quality in Salt Lake City. A scientist at heart, I jumped at the opportunity to run up and down a mountain as many times as I could in a designated timeframe to raise money for education and projects dedicated to eliminating pollution. My good friend Vince Heyd agreed to do the six-hour event with me, and our aim was for three times up and down Grandeur Peak.

Heading into the event was emotional. It took place about six months after my initial injuries, when I had completely let go of the idea that I would ever compete or run again. Now I was wearing a bib number and running with about 200 other people.

I was happy but completely terrified. How would I stack up? It wasn't a race—I knew that—but that competitive side is hard to turn off, and when that gun rang out in the crisp air, my anxious race nerves kicked into adrenaline. I started to run/power-hike uphill as fast as I could, Vince on my heels.

Snow fell thickly on the ground in big flakes flurrying from the sky. The ground became a mix of snow and mud, and we didn't have the best traction. My foot was sore due to the temperature change. *Or maybe from the loose screw?* I thought. I couldn't move as fast as I wanted to. I felt held back by the physical pain and the pressure of wanting to race and knowing I couldn't. That pressure became a weight, and only fifteen minutes into the race it bubbled out in tears streaming down my face.

At a steep switchback, I pulled off the trail, tears clouding my vision. Deep, sad tears for the loss of my competitive self, for wanting to push myself and knowing I wasn't ready. I was crying because I was happy to even be out here. I was crying for letting down Vince, for letting down myself—I wanted to do this for fun anyway. I turned to Vince, who had pulled off the trail with me. "I'm sorry, Vince. I don't know what's wrong with me. I don't know why I'm crying!" I knew it was a gift to have gotten to this point in my recovery but being there, in that "race" setting . . . I didn't feel like myself.

As I said those words to Vince he said, "Hill, it's OK! You're doing great!" He gave me a deep, understanding hug. A hug that communicated friendship, support, and acceptance. "Let's have some fun and enjoy the snow!" I wiped the tears from my face, and with them let go of the pressure of wanting to race (and knowing I couldn't). Now I could just embrace the fun time with my friend.

As we started back up the trail again, Vince started singing. First it was "rap-singing" his favorite Eminem songs. I couldn't help but laugh (and was also impressed by how good he was!). From that moment on, the expectation shifted. We spent the day laughing, singing, eating pierogies, and downing a shot of Fireball each time we summited the top of Grandeur Peak. Vince bestowed upon me my very own rapper name, "Loose Screw," as I too began to rap and sing aloud to my favorite songs. Together our laughs and lyrics echoed over the trails, passing our joy on to other runners as we passed by them.

As evening arrived, the snow started to freeze, but we put on our microspikes and pressed on. At the close of the event we had logged three laps for a total of nineteen miles. Vince and I jogged around the parking lot until we hit twenty miles. My biggest outing since nearly dying. I believed it was only the beginning.

I knew I faced surgery and yet another recovery when I came home. But my belief in myself was stronger than ever. Even if I never returned to racing, I could run again. I had done it and I believed it. It was more about the journey to get there, the community, the memories, the struggles. It was about the greater purpose of what running could do for others, what it could do for me, how it could push my own boundaries, and how I could constantly learn from each experience on a new mountain or trail.

But through all of this, belief is what pulled me through. Belief that required a quiet strength to cut through the deepest lows and demand resilience. It might not have been at the forefront of my mind every day, but belief was there: belief in myself, and the hard work I was putting in. My belief was restored that day in Utah, and I was ready for the next chapter of my recovery. Ready to engage with the unknown and believe that anything was possible. In the face of imperfection, setback, or surprise, I believed that a positive outlook and perspective could shape any outcome into a good one. It wouldn't be easy or uncomplicated, but I had the mentality to meet the challenge head-on.

6 PATIENCE TAKES PRACTICE

I'm not patient. I hate waiting. I'm like a wild mustang (someone once told me that). Like that mustang, I'm someone who doesn't know what a fence is or what boundaries are—and just wants that cowboy to get the fuck off my back. I want to be free. Unbridled. Untamed.

Injuries, however, force us to relinquish freedom, and they require extreme patience. A constant push-and-pull battle rages as you drive yourself within the boundaries of each stage of recovery—to pull back a little bit so you don't do more damage but push just enough to promote healing and mitigate losses. It's a battle of the mind and will, and it's a process—certainly not a linear one.

Progress often involves setbacks. *It's a process.* I repeated this to myself in those moments of perpetual impatience, longing to move again, to race again, seething for competition, pining for the feeling of sweat dripping down my face and my lungs and legs burning. I clung to belief that one day it would come.

It's a process.

I had to embrace that fact, along with the uncertainty that comes with it. In the meantime, I visualized myself slaying all the bitches on the trail. (Yes, I say this to myself when I'm racing—an altered competitive ego that wants to slay all the ladies out there. I love them, my competitors; they're strong women who absolutely crush. But on the trail, during a race, I want to beat, nay, crush every single one of them. "Slay all the bitches"—said with love, of course.)

I visualized leaving them so far behind on the climbs and bombing down the descents that only the memory of my footsteps remained in their path. I tasted it. I wanted that feeling so badly. Right. Now.

I will get it. Soon.

It's a process, I kept repeating.

Do what you can now.

It's time to go to the gym.

I discovered Revo Physiotherapy and Sports Performance, in Boulder, about four weeks after my accident. This gym is for the best athletes, professionals who go to prepare for their season in sport, and everyone swore by their team of specialists when they were injured and needed help.

When I scooted through the sliding glass doors that first day, the first thing I noticed was *a lot* of people on crutches. I didn't feel like I stuck out in the crowd. In fact, I felt right at home, like I fit in. My scooter almost seemed normal to have in this place. The gym was an open floor plan, with a turf football field on the left side. A high school ski team was pushing sleds across the turf, then sprinting back once they completed a lap up and down the field. I watched their movement longingly before I continued to scoot through the gym, trying to stay out of the way.

The rest of the gym held free weights, squat racks, stationary bikes, and other gym equipment I didn't recognize. I hadn't been to a gym like this since my college tennis days. I began to feel a bit self-conscious and discouraged by my predicament, uneasy and unsure as to why I had even come here, and turned my scooter around. That's when a physical therapist named Matt Smith came over to me and introduced himself. "You must be Hillary," he said with a big smile.

"How could you tell?" I asked, cracking a smile, if only to hold back the inevitable tears. At that moment, I felt intensely vulnerable yet accepted. Matt gently put his hand on my back. "Welcome. Let me show you around the gym and tell you a bit about what we're all about." After chatting and scooting about the gym for about forty-five minutes, I knew I had found the right place. A balance of cutting-edge recovery, community, and good people.

I started going to Revo every day, consulting with Matt on basic strength exercises, and then incrementally building up as my recovery progressed and I could do more activities.

I had a love-hate relationship with the gym. I loved how strong I could feel, learning how much weight my muscles can handle. I loved the community I created at Revo. I had my own team there, most significantly Matt, without whom I would have never gotten back to running. I loved getting out of my house and being able to move my body, no matter how limited I was at first.

But I *hated* working out inside. I hated feeling like a bumbling idiot, searching for the correct weights to use, or not knowing how to do a proper squat or deadlift. I hated being constantly corrected—my form was crap when I first started. I hated that I needed help with everything. It was demoralizing. I might be a professional runner, but I certainly wasn't a professional weight lifter, and I was humbled by my beginner skills.

Despite these setbacks, hesitations, and frustration, I kept going. Matt, Dane, Brian, and all the PTs and owners at Revo became my extended family. We all worked together, invested in each other's success. I was there every day at first, and then twice a day. The gym kept me motivated and gave me purpose. It felt like my home. I even joked with the guys, like I lived there.

In the beginning, I was still using my scooter and couldn't bear weight, so we started small, focusing on mobility. Stretching and testing the range of motion of my left ankle. This one wasn't broken, but it had been severely twisted, and its mobility was limited. My calves, tight and weakened thanks to limited motion and altered weight-bearing, needed to be stretched. I also did mobility and stretching exercises for my wrists. My hands were extremely weak since I couldn't use them. I could barely pick up or grip anything without them becoming sore and losing my grip. I squeezed foam balls and lifted baby weights, trying to regain strength.

This was the very beginning, and the exercises were so simple. Too simple. I longed to do more. I wanted to sweat, to do a workout that made my legs ache and my lungs burn. Instead, I was stuck indoors working on mobility or doing aqua jogging.

That was the other half of my day. In the pool, where I could bob up and down a swimming lane, trying not to drown while simultaneously working on my running form. I hated it at first. It was so boring, monotonous, and slow. But somehow I began to look forward to that time out of the house. I began to crave it. The slow process of ordering an Uber, loading myself in the car, and engaging in the inevitable conversation with the driver on the ride to the recreation center, where the staff members now knew me by name. I'd smile at them through the glass doors as I pushed the handicapped button to open the doors. By the time I reached the front desk to scan my card, they already had the elevator key waiting for me. "How are you today, Hillary? You here for a swim?" I'd smile, exchange some pleasant small talk, and take the elevator down one floor to enter the locker room.

I'd change into my swimsuit, put on my aqua jogging belt, and meticulously strip off my arm casts. Then I'd gently, and very slowly, scoot out to the pool area. I didn't want to slip on the wet linoleum floor.

On this particular day, Aaron was on duty. He was a student at University of Colorado Boulder, and was working at the rec center to earn some extra money while he studied mechanical engineering. I talked with him a bit before I started the always nerve-wracking process of leaving my scooter by the guardrails as I lowered myself down to my butt and entered the water. Once in the water, I could make my way through the shallows to the deep end.

"How long will it be today, Hillary?" Aaron asked.

"I'm not sure yet. I need to see how I feel." I put in my wireless headphones and began bobbing up and down, moving my legs and arms in a running motion under the water, slowly making my way to the other end of the pool.

This process, however painstakingly long and arduous, was a form of self-care. Every obstacle and annoyance I overcame to get myself into that pool was a representation of how much I was caring for and about myself. That shift in perspective was what allowed me to keep coming back, and to even look forward to those slow, boring laps in the pool.

About four months into my recovery, when Dr. Gorman cleared me to do more weight-bearing, I graduated from aqua jogging to the Airdyne. This exercise bike requires your arms too, so it was a good alternative to developing my hand strength and starting to push on my right leg. Matt was there to make sure I didn't go too hard too soon.

Matt and my coach Adam communicated with me a lot during that time to make sure I stayed on track, both physically and emotionally. They could both tell I was struggling immensely with holding back and being patient. Matt added strength workouts to my routine so I could practice squatting with more weight, as well as a lot of banded work for hip and glute strength to mitigate as much muscle loss as possible. It was important to maintain good hip strength—it's the powerhouse for all things running. I was surprised by how much body-weight and banded exercises did to maintain my muscle integrity and strength.

When I was cleared to start walking without my boot around the fifth month of recovery, I was thrilled to get outside again. I used trekking poles to stabilize myself, because my definition of hiking meant a steep, rocky trail—something I don't think Dr. Gorman realized when she told me I could start hiking.

Free of the boot, I loved to start the day with a sunrise hike. At first it was a few days a week, then every other day. But soon enough I was out there every day. Some days the hikes were shorter than others, based on the pain and swelling of my foot, and I had to be choosy with my trail selection because the Colorado winter meant ice. I always carried microspikes in my pack so if I came across any ice, I would be safe.

Getting outside was really important to me. It freshened up my routine and gave me renewed hope that I could get back to moving in the mountains. Every sunrise hike was special, even if it was on the same trail I had hiked the day before. This was where I greeted the day and set my intentions. It was a special start between me and Mother Nature.

After the early-morning hike, I'd make my way to my favorite coffee shop, where the baristas encouraged me and the progress I had made. These same baristas had been behind the counter all those days when I came in on my scooter and could hardly turn around in the shop, balancing my coffee in the front basket. So, the reality that I was now walking and hiking . . . it was encouraging for us all.

I still walked with the limp, but it slowly grew better through diligent work in the gym, my sessions with Levi, and using my trekking poles. By the sixth month of recovery I was hiking even more and had even progressed to a hike/jog, trotting down the trail with the help of my poles.

I developed a love-hate relationship with those trekking poles. I wanted so badly to ditch them and just run, but I knew my body wasn't ready for that yet. The poles were becoming extensions of me, keeping me safe and stable as the muscles in my feet and ankles began to stabilize again.

Running is really a series of jumps, so I had to practice that in the gym and get really good at it if I wanted to lose those poles. But when I jumped, it still wasn't even and balanced. I needed to regain trust in my right foot and ensure I used it correctly. If I favored it, and landed more on the left side, that foot would get sore. I began to notice compensation issues on the left side and had to consciously think about the correct foot strike and place-ment on my right side with every jump and step.

Working through this with Levi I developed a sort of mantra for when I was hiking or jogging downhill. "Find your big toe," I'd say as I moved through a step. But all the progress seemed to come crashing down when Dr. Gorman told me I needed that surgery to remove the screws in my right foot.

Even though we had discussed removing the hardware in my foot at some point, I hadn't expected it so soon. When I learned that surgery was imminent, my thoughts flew immediately to my new-found routine. I had just begun to find my stride and was finally able to go outside again. It was disappointing and discour-aging to think about having to start all over again.

The surgery was routine enough, but I would still go under anesthesia, and although I'd be able to walk right away, hiking or any sort of impact (like jumping) was off the table for a while. Accepting this was like another punch to the gut. But then I remembered something.

It's a process.

Even though it was not perfect, it was a step in the right direc-tion, and it was necessary to get back to full function of my foot.

On the morning of February 14th, 2018, my screws were removed—well, at least what they could get out. One part of the screw was left inside the bone in my foot—it's still there now—since it had broken off. The doctors got out what they could and left a little piece for me to remember them by. The morning of the surgery, I wrote a little ode to my soon-to-be ex, the screws.

To my dearest screws:
You came into my life, abruptly.
Holding me together, firmly.

While we started out slow,
It was only until I got into the flow;

And I've certainly tried my best,
Putting you both to the test.

Now one of you is broken,
So I'm taking you both out as a token

Of my gratitude and faith.

That this operation will help me rise above,
So I can return to what I love.

When I went back to Revo shortly after the surgery, Matt had me back to the basics, doing my hip strength and mobility exercises and core work. It was difficult to not view it as a step backward. I felt like all my hard work from the previous months was forgotten, that I had nothing to show for it and was regressing. But Matt and my coach Adam reminded me that wasn't true. In reality, the fact that I had been doing so much, and in such good form, before the surgery would only help my recovery. Make it

INJURIES FORCE US TO RELINQUISH FREEDOM. THEY REQUIRE EXTREME PATIENCE.

faster. I could only hope they were right.

One day when I got to the gym Matt was smiling and positive as usual—a stark contrast to myself. Still bummed and feeling stuck in my lack of mobility once again, I wasn't having such a good day. I went into the gym, knowing that just seeing Matt and the team would brighten my outlook.

Something was different about Matt that day though. He wasn't in his normal workout clothes. I almost didn't recognize him in the patterned sweater he wore. I had never seen him outside of his gym clothes, and something about seeing him this way immediately brought a smile to my face.

It reminded me that Matt, too, was a real person outside of his role as my PT. Somehow that sweater with its tribal grey, blue, and red pattern represented his life outside of the gym and our therapy sessions, and my respect for him grew. Matt was showing up for me, and all the people in his life, in and outside of work.

I greeted Matt with a big hug (per usual). "Nice sweater, Matt. I really like it," I said with a grin. Maybe something was wrong with my tone, because he didn't believe me and thought I was poking fun. I *am* a pretty sarcastic person and make fun of the people I love most, so he did have a point, but this time I was being genuine. As I reassured him that I really did like the sweater and his "business casual" gym look, he laughed, still unbelieving.

"Today and this sweater . . . everyone is commenting on it! I'm never wearing regular clothes to the gym again." We both laughed, and that small moment brightened my lousy day.

The next day was another bad one. My foot hurt, and I couldn't do squats like I had before the surgery. My foot and ankle were swollen, impeding my range of motion.

As I was lifting weights, doing a squat, the tears spilled over. Matt came over to offer encouragement to keep going and to correct my form and hip position, as he always did. We had been working together for a while. Rearranging my hips to correct the movement, or reminding me to put myself in the right position, was a simple routine. "Get your hips back," was all he had to say as he walked by, and I'd adjust, appreciating the reminder.

On this day, however, he took his time. "You know how to do this. Your body knows how," Matt said. "It's just healing again, and you need to give it a little patience. You'll be stronger for it. Recovery is not a linear path. These setbacks are necessary for progress." With his words, he reminded me I could do this, that it was hard for a reason, and that I was strong enough to meet it head-on.

I managed to continue with my workout. As I was doing my mobility exercises and getting ready to go home, Matt came over again.

"So, you really liked that sweater yesterday, huh?"

I cracked a smile. "Yes, Matt, I wasn't making fun of you," I said shyly. "I thought you looked good in it. You should be business-casual more often."

With a laugh, he said, "Thanks, Hill," his tone kind and warm. "The sweater is yours, Hill. On one condition—it's yours after you win your first race back." We had a deal.

I realized Matt was right. I needed that second surgery to become strong again. It was all part of the process to make me whole, as an athlete but also as a person. Setbacks are part of the endgame, and getting to a goal is never straightforward. There are always stumbling blocks and unexpected obstacles that must be overcome in order to achieve that goal.

Although I was familiar with this mentality when it came to meeting a deadline for graduate school or writing a term paper, it was harder to come to terms with in my physical and emotional recovery. When I started on this journey, I felt an immense amount of uncertainty. Would I would ever run again, move again in the mountains? Was I going to be in pain all the time? Would I be emotionally scarred from the experience?

I had to make a choice each day to accept those uncertainties and fear and keep moving anyway. It's like going to a place you've never been before and turning off the lights, then walking around in the dark to reach the other side of the room. You have to bump into things to find out where they are and go slowly enough that those bumps don't hurt you too much.

It's about embracing the unknown and still choosing to move forward. I had to have that approach with my recovery. Physically, I wasn't sure if I was going to be a professional athlete anymore, or if I could make a full recovery, but I accepted that uncertainty and worked every day with the intention of running again. Emotionally, I had to embrace all the ups and downs and work on redefining my self-worth and relationship with myself.

It wasn't about being able to win again, or even being an elite again. Sure, I enjoyed the competition and proving to myself I was strong and could run fast. But winning a race, as good as it feels, is only a temporary high—fleeting. I was chasing this feeling early in my running career, as many young, competitive athletes do. Even when I achieved those goals—won races, set course records—the first question that reporters or interviewers or even my running peers would ask was, "What's next?"

No time was awarded to celebrate the accomplishment or revel in the beauty of the achievement I had just completed. Everyone was always looking to the next thing, preparing for the next bigger, longer, more difficult race. No wonder people get burned out on this stuff or are addicted to winning, only to sacrifice their integrity or who they are to go after a win—after win, after win, after win.

I recognized this burnout potential early on in my running career. As a competitive person, and with experience from playing tennis in my college years, I knew that it was possible to get burned out on something you love. So, when I first started running and racing, I was extra cautious to not make it solely about the competition, but to enjoy the process of moving and training. To enjoy even the tough days and difficult workouts, the times when running didn't feel good. It's important to understand those lows so you also know what it feels like to have a wonderful day spent running, where everything clicks and feels flawless and right.

When I was faced with the idea of never running or competing again at a professional level, I told myself that I needed to make peace with that possibility. I had to be a complete person, a whole person, a happy person, in the absence of competition, racing, or professional sponsorship.

Accepting this didn't happen instantly, and there was a lot of grieving involved. Lots of self-pity and questioning, "Why did this happen to me?" But, eventually, things started to flow, and I began working toward my goals of movement and happiness, separate from competition or a need to be an elite runner again. I started my recovery to become a better person, separate from my athletic goals and pursuits. It was for *me,* not for running. If I was ever going to run again, I wanted to rediscover the beauty of that process and movement, rediscover the reason why I ever wanted to run in the first place, separate from competition.

It wasn't about letting go of my competitive edge or giving up that part of myself. I am super competitive and always will be. It's not something I can change; it's ingrained in my DNA and expressed in even the most mundane tasks, like getting ready in the morning (How fast can I be showered and out the door after a run?), cooking dinner (Can I be done in time to catch my favorite show?), tackling to-do lists (How many things can I get done before 7 a.m.?).

There's no lack of competitive spirit within me, but what there isn't enough of is patience to enjoy the process and let go of the expectations and end goals associated with my competitive nature. Just because I didn't get everything done on my to-do list, it doesn't mean I'm a failure or undeserving of patience, grace, and a little forgiveness.

This was one of the most important things I learned, and it's something I continue to practice every day. Patience takes practice and it's not perfect; therein lies the beauty. Winning is great. Being prepared is wonderful. I really enjoy it, but it's predictable, finite, and dull.

The reason I like running, and even racing, is that you never know what lies ahead. It's just like going into that dark room and fumbling around until you get a mental picture of the obstacles that lie in front of you. It's about problem-solving; getting to the finish line is only possible if you confront the unknown head-on. That's beautiful. I wanted to experience that again. Not the act of running, but the beautiful puzzle of the process. All those experiences bring life to the process.

Experiencing my injury, multiple surgeries, and recovery gave me the chance to learn about myself again. To rediscover what made me feel most alive and whole and a part of this world. I knew running had a lot to do with it, but I wasn't sure exactly how it contributed, and I was letting the emphasis on competition muddy the waters and contaminate the reasons I loved running in the first place. So, in a way, I was thankful for my recovery. It was an opportunity to learn, to grow, and to become a new, more complete person—a more complete runner. I got to fall in love with the imperfect process all over again.

Matt reminded me of this time and time again. He helped me get through some tough lows, constantly encouraging me and telling me I was "putting in the work" here, in the present. "It doesn't matter how it pays off," he would say. "It will pay off in the end, somehow."

He knew I wanted to get back out there and compete. Why else would he offer me his super cool sweater as a gift for my first win back? But that offer was more a gesture, an act of encouragement to keep trying, no matter the endpoint.

I would still be the same me whether I won another race or lost or decided to never compete again. The result wasn't a reflection on me as a person. What I did need to do was give it an honest try and find out what I was made of throughout the process. It was worth it to try, and risk failing, because every day that I showed up to do the work, I proved to myself that I was enough as I was, in the here and now: injured, recovering, working toward a goal, competing, or never competing again. I was worth just as much as I was before the injury, and before my second surgery.

The stylish new sweater would merely represent the significance of a win or a return to racing. It was something I could wear on a crisp fall morning in Colorado, reflecting on the process, knowing where I'd been to get to the now.

7 YOU CAN ACHIEVE IT, NOT ATTAIN IT

I used to think that recovery was very straightforward. That you achieve certain benchmarks and keep progressing, keep improving, until there are no more setbacks, and everything is fine again—forgotten, like new. Of course, this isn't the case unless a person is either in denial or blissfully unaware.

I sometimes catch myself in disbelief of my own experience, wondering if I ever was in Norway, and if I did, indeed, survive that accident. Did it really happen? All I have to do is trace the ridges of scars that speckle my body to know it wasn't a nightmare but a reality. I like to think things happen for a reason, though. I like to think I have some direction in determining what that reason is. Of course, I don't know the reason right away, but I do know that the things in life I enjoy most are usually the most difficult.

Whether it's the type of races I choose (skyrunning) or the profession I pursue (neuroscientist to professional athlete) or how I learn (the hard way, every single time), I enjoy going after things with all my heart and effort. Even if it ends with failure, at least I'll learn something.

I spent the better part of the year post-accident not feeling like myself. I felt like a part of me was lost, and there was a hole somewhere. Something was missing, but I couldn't define what it was. I was experiencing rebirth, a rediscovery of self. And an inevitable side effect, at least for me, was the feeling of losing myself, and not knowing who I was or who I would become. Like a big jigsaw puzzle, all of the pieces were there . . . I just needed to figure out how to put them together again. It took time.

I started seeing a counselor through all this. My thoughts were a jumble in my head, and I needed a way to get them out, to express myself and talk about the changes I was going through. I had gone through a physical trauma, yes, but the deeper cuts were the emotional wounds I was attempting to navigate. I am no expert, so I sought the help of one. That's when I met Timothy Tate.

Timothy doesn't define himself as a therapist. When we met, he spoke of himself as an elder, and a psychotherapist, whose main role is to help others navigate their inner shadows and realize their self-worth again. I met Timothy through The North Face and a team captain at the time, Conrad Anker. Conrad and Timothy were dear friends and had worked together for many years, helping each other through life's challenging moments.

Conrad, a climber and alpinist, had experienced trauma on many levels throughout his career and knew the importance of confronting his demons to be able to do the sports, and profession, he loved. Conrad was the one who pushed for Timothy to be hired to work with the athletes on The North Face team to work through the traumas of the mountain accidents that so many athletes have experienced, including losing loved ones in those same circumstances.

After getting in touch with Timothy and having some initial phone calls, I flew to Bozeman, Montana, to begin our work. I had been to a therapist before and knew the importance of talk therapy, but Timothy was different. The moment I met him in person and gave him a hug, I instantly felt a warmth and supportiveness. A tall man, with wispy white hair and a big, bushy, white mustache, he looked like a modern-day cowboy, with a glowing smile and this look in his eyes that told you he had so many stories to tell.

We sat down in his office and just started talking. Over nothing in particular, the conversation just flowed. We were learning about one another, how we thought about problems, how we solved them, how we enjoyed the natural world. Tim asked me a lot of questions about what happened in my life, to get me to where I am today. Of course, my accident played a role in this, but he wanted a more complete explanation and image of who I was as a person. It wasn't one-sided though; Timothy encouraged me to open up by using examples from his own experiences and showing me the strength there is in vulnerability.

I shared about my accident and what was going on in my life in the present. At that point, I was post–second surgery to remove my screws and getting back into my run/jog routine, but I was struggling, finding it difficult to feel normal again—not even knowing what normal meant to me anymore.

I fought to maintain posture and poise. I felt like I should be strong, together, happy. I was moving again. I was alive, recovering—but I felt empty. I felt pressured by what I "should" be, when in reality I didn't know who I wanted to be or how to feel the depth of emotions that come with a trauma like mine.

"You can cry," Timothy encouraged me. "Don't be afraid. You don't have to know why you're crying or what you're feeling. Just release it."

"I'm afraid I'll never be the same again," I finally told him. "I'm afraid I've lost who I was. I don't know who I am anymore."

"Well, yeah! Of course you're not the same!" Timothy replied. "You're different, you're evolving. That's what makes this process wonderful. You're not the same person as before. You've outgrown her." There was no judgment or forcefulness in his tone. He wasn't in a hurry to make me realize the inevitable changes in myself. He was simply there with me, ready to help guide me there.

I flew home to Boulder a couple days after our first meeting, but Timothy and I continued to talk by phone. The more I shared with him, the more my vulnerability grew. Not many people really see me like that. I do a good job at keeping that part of me tucked away and wrapped up safely. I have a lot of friends, but very few see the real me, stripped down, as someone who's not always smiling, someone who doubts, questions, and demands the best of herself no matter the cost. Timothy was beginning to understand what made me tick, and he saw the inner turmoil I was experiencing as I battled my old self, and my self-imposed expectations, with the discovery of my new self, accepting the unknown and the changes that came with it.

I began to accept that I would never be the same. I knew this at the basic level . . . how could I be the same after what had happened? Past experiences shift current perspective and set new precedents for how you react to current and future situations. This was certainly the case for me.

I met my first serious boyfriend Riccardo while I was living in Spain during my semester abroad. He was Italian, and we fell madly in love and ended up dating long-distance for a year after I moved back to the United States. We eventually broke up because that long distance was weighing on both of us. But now when I look to date someone, my past experience with Riccardo makes me think twice about long-distance relationships and what's realistic.

Past experience = perspective shift = new precedent.

Why was this so hard for me to accept when it came to my accident and the ensuing trauma it afflicted upon me? I was resisting change and wanted to hold on to what made me feel most like myself before the accident, without truly understanding how I had outgrown this and was setting new dimensions for myself.

One of the main themes Timothy and I discussed was self-acceptance and the liberation that comes with accepting yourself as you are, even in your imperfectness—the struggle, the change, and the rediscovery. I have trouble with this. I'm a perfectionist at my core, with an insane work ethic. I don't let things happen; I *make* them happen. When I want something, I find a way to get it done, and I do it well. I hold myself to a very high standard. Sometimes that standard is unrealistic and impossible to meet, but I keep it that way, so I don't slack off.

I shared with Timothy how these traits had manifested in my life and what I had achieved. How I picked up tennis my freshman year of high school and earned a scholarship to play in college by my senior year. I shared how I wanted to study abroad in Spain, all while majoring in chemistry, playing collegiate tennis, participating in student government, and working part-time. I was advised to choose, to compromise. Instead, I found a way to do it all, and I ended up with a double major in Spanish and chemistry. I shared how I found trail running during graduate school and loved it so much that within my first year of competing I had already gained a sponsorship.

I wasn't familiar with the term "acceptance." In fact, I affiliated this word with slowing down or settling for second best. I wanted nothing to do with that. I needed to constantly achieve and strive to be my best. Although that's a good quality to have, in order to do it, I felt I needed to trick myself into achieving. I kept telling myself that I wasn't good enough, ever, in order to put in the necessary work to be the best that I could be. It was the story I told myself constantly, and frankly, it was exhausting. As I shared this with Timothy, I could feel his empathy just by looking into his kind eyes looking back at me.

"Hillary," he said quietly, "you don't need to do this to yourself. Have you ever thought about accepting yourself as you are right

THERE IS NOTHING ABOUT YOU THAT IS MEDIOCRE. YOU ARE EXCEPTIONAL IN EVERYTHING YOU DO. THAT'S PART OF YOU. IT'S INGRAINED IN YOUR DNA.

here and now? That you are good enough—perfect in fact—just as you are? What would happen if you did that?"

I fell silent. Just the thought of it felt like settling. I shifted uncomfortably as I pondered the question. I didn't know what to say. What would that look like? Would I suddenly become complacent, lazy, devoid of motivation, and strive for nothing? My thoughts began to spiral wildly.

"I don't know!" I finally burst out. "Wouldn't that be giving up on myself? To accept myself in mediocrity?"

Timothy smiled and said gently, "Oh, Hillary, there is nothing about you that is mediocre. You are exceptional in everything you do. That's part of you. It's ingrained in your DNA. You are going to try your best at everything you do. Accepting yourself as you are isn't going to change that. It's only going to help you get out of your own way. Accepting yourself for the light and fire that you have only can make the fire grow more. What you are doing with self-doubt, and tricking yourself into not believing in your own power, is stifling that flame, depriving it of oxygen so it can only grow so big. Self-acceptance, believing that you are indeed perfect—and I use that word purposefully . . . I'll say it again, that you are perfect—as you are, is the only real way to self-enlightenment. You won't forget to work hard and strive for your best, because that's innate within you. That's who you are. That's part of what makes you perfect."

I had never thought about myself in this way before. His descriptions awed me. It made sense, and his logic was sound. I was the only thing holding myself back from being the best version of me I could be. It was self-acceptance that I was missing all along.

These many conversations with Timothy surrounding certain "shadows" or stories that I tell myself to keep me from being the best version of myself are what started me on my path to self-acceptance and growth. It certainly was not immediate or natural for me. It was difficult and required constant work. My habitually self-deprecating thoughts had almost become automatic, so it took (and still takes) a lot of patience and time to work on this. But even in a few short months of my new practice of self-acceptance, letting myself be perfect in my imperfections, I saw huge improvements in my life.

Problem-solving became easier, and I began to trust myself again. I started to rely on and take care of myself, no matter what problem was thrown my way. "I got you, Hill," I would whisper aloud, reassuring myself in times of doubt and wavering. It was a continual practice, and one I continue to work on today.

But my work with Timothy didn't end there. During this particular discussion, Timothy and I examined the theme of my return to running. I was getting stronger and stronger, and my hike/runs were starting to look more like runs. Still, I was using air quotes to describe my "runs" to my friends and coach. I knew they were runs, and so did they, but I wanted to protect myself. I was protecting myself from my own expectations and those of everyone around me. I was beginning to feel ready to start running for real . . . but at the same time, I still didn't feel ready at all.

Timothy saw my hesitation and wanted to address it right away. He recognized my competitiveness and my extremely motivated spirit. He knew it was only a matter of time before I would want to run, and then to start competing again.

I told him what my fears were, explained my hesitations . . . but Timothy didn't buy it. "What are you really afraid of?" he asked. "What is really holding you back?"

"I'm afraid I won't be the same again," I confessed. "I'm afraid of being disappointed."

This fear is tough for athletes. Athletes are constantly achieving and striving for faster times, better results, year after year after year, like a linear progression. As if there's only one way to get better and improve and become faster.

The clock doesn't lie; I like that about running. It's brutally honest. If, from one year to the next, I run the same course and win it both years, but my time is slower the second year, didn't I get worse? If you look at it logically, yes, absolutely. But there are other factors to consider. How hot was it? How was the competition? Was there another lady gunning at my heels, pushing me to go faster, or was I leading easily the whole time? Was the trail muddy or dry? How did I feel mentally? Emotionally? I can logically work my way through these explanations and understand how, from year to year, courses vary and, justifiably, so do the times athletes run them in.

Why couldn't I do that for myself? I wasn't the same person I was before my accident. I would never be. So why was I chasing the old part of me, the old times I had run, the old goals I had? I had evolved. I had changed. I was different now, and that wasn't a bad thing.

Timothy and I discussed the danger of the "comeback." How it was suffocating and set constraints and boundaries on my recovery and evolution as a human. I hated the word too. To me, it represented a finality to my story. That once I had "come back" and started to run again or do a race, my journey was over, and it was time to stop growing or striving to be better. I wasn't the same, so there was nothing to come back to. The target was constantly shifting.

But I was still afraid of not being the same Hillary. Not only in the eyes of the public or my sponsors, but in my own eyes. I was afraid I would let myself down if I decided to run and it didn't feel the same, or if I couldn't run fast again. We explored this fear and my relationship to competition, starting with my favorite run around my home in Boulder, Shadow Canyon to South Boulder Peak.

"How many times have you run this route?" Timothy asked.

"At least fifty times last year," I said.

"How many of those runs were the same? I'm not speaking about the time it took you to do it, but I'm talking about the weather, how you felt during the run, what you experienced?"

"None of them," I replied. "Every run was different. In fact, that's what I love about trail running the most, that every time I go out for a run, even on the same trail, it's different. The sights, the sounds, the smells, how I felt, how I moved, what I saw, what I thought about." I started smiling as I described it.

Timothy gazed at me and said, "Then how can you be afraid of not being the same when that's the thing you love most about running?"

His question that day made me think about running in a different way, and it gave me the courage to start trying. No matter the result. I could let go of expectation and try for the sake of trying, to discover something new.

I started to invite my friends to go on my runs with me. I started to be less afraid of the end result, and I rediscovered the joy the movement of running gave me. I realized I had begun placing too much emphasis on the end result, or a time or place in a race. Running a race was more about how I'd stack up against the competition than about the course itself or the beauty of the terrain.

I think this happens to a lot of professional athletes. The results can get the best of them. But my recovery reminded me why I started running in the first place. It wasn't for a sponsorship or race win or record. I ran so much and trained so hard because I loved it. I loved the good days just as much as I loved the bad ones. I trusted the imperfect journey that running took me on. But when I became sponsored and started traveling and racing more, I began to lose sight of that joy. Especially on competition day. There were glimpses of that joy during my training and in the buildup to races, but the races had started to become stressful, and I had begun to doubt my abilities.

Coming out on the other side of my accident, thinking about what running again would mean for returning to competitive running and racing, I didn't want to feel stifled. I didn't want to race or run just because I felt pressure to be the same as I was before. I wanted to run for the sake of running and the joy, pain, suffering, and happiness it brought me. I wanted to run because I felt like the best version of myself with it in my life.

One of the lasting comments Timothy made in one of our wonderful discussions was this:

You can achieve it, but not attain it.

It was the advice a mentor and confidant had given him years ago. At first when he said this to me, I was infuriated by it. I wanted to achieve it *and* attain it. I wanted something to hold on to, to show for my hard work—proof of my accomplishments. But this is rather selfish and naïve. I know from first-hand experience that even winning a race is fleeting. It's done and over in an instant. As soon as you cross the finishing tape with your hands up, it's over, the moment gone. There's nothing to hold on to but the memories or photos of the event. Maybe the trophy will bring back that fleeting feeling, but it's never the same. Even in a great achievement, there's no attaining anything.

Although I realized this irony, I still didn't like it. I still held on to trophies and looked at old photos of races, trying to imagine what it would feel like to run again, and maybe even win. I wanted to bottle up the feeling, hold it close, keep it warm and safe, and go to sleep with it at night. But the real beauty lies in the achievement, not the attainment, of a goal. Trying to hold on to the achievement lessens the value of the achievement itself, and can even blemish it. The enjoyment is in the process and celebration of the achievement and what it represents. It can never be recreated or reformed, because then it would become something new and different. In order to really achieve something, there is no attainment. It's gone the moment you reach the achievement.

It seems like an endless loop, a labyrinth you can never get out of. That's the perspective I had at first. But the more I thought about it, and the more I understood what the phrase really meant, the more I discovered its beauty, and the less constricted I felt by certain boundaries I had set up in my life. You can achieve it, but not attain it. To me, the inability to attain any achievement meant the ultimate freedom to explore, to learn, grow, and experience all this life has to offer. Every setback, twist, and turn on life's journey, every new goal and achievement I set before myself became an opportunity to be creative, to learn, and to become better.

This perspective shift, which is ongoing, gave me the courage to start running again, no matter what it looked like. I began to believe in myself again, and to embrace the fear of the unknown. It was out of my control. I didn't need to hold on to everything so tightly, or long for control over every situation (of course, I'm still working on this one too). I discovered that if I held on too tightly it would ruin the very moment I was trying to keep.

I began to embrace the uncertainties that life, and my return to running, would inevitably bring. Instead of searching for something to grasp on to—to attain—I could explore the moment, here and now, and experience the joys of the simple movement of running. I could experience the pain and doubt, and instead of judging it or clinging to that negativity, I could accept it as part of the course, a necessary experience to bring me closer to my recovery and myself. Thus, any goal or achievement thereafter would be a representation of my hard work and dedication, a celebration of my passion for something I love. I would not want to hang on to that, to wrap it up into one discrete package, because doing so would ruin the achievement. I now had the tools to begin running again and to start living my life to its fullest potential, embracing each imperfect part of me along the way.

HONOR YOUR PROCESS 8

"Anger, doubt, fear—all of these are a part of the process.

Feel them, let them run their course. And trust that you will,

as ever, land on your feet. Even if one of them is pretty hurt

at the moment and the brain attached to it is spinning."

—DAVID POWDER STEELE

One of the best things about injury and recovery is the extra time it gives you. Trust me, I can't believe I just wrote that, and what's even more impressive is that I never thought I'd actually mean it when I said it.

Time is the most valuable currency we have. We can't get it back, and it seems that we always want more of it. I've noticed that the things I love most in life also require a lot of it. It's the main way I show I care about something or someone: giving my time.

But let's talk more about believing that the extra time you get after an injury is a gift, not a curse. I can be a bit too devoted to my schedule, easily caught up in my to-do list, going through life perpetually busy, and making sure to squeeze in everything I need to do each day. Training and running are huge time commitments, especially for an endurance athlete, and it takes constant planning and scheduling to accomplish a successful training plan.

There comes a time when training becomes stressful, especially from the standpoint of time. It becomes a chore or an obligation. On many occasions I've heard long-distance runners say, "I'm just 'getting it in' or 'getting it done.'" Instead of focusing on the quality or enjoyment of the sport you love, it turns into a numbers game that has you stressing and obsessing about volume, hours, and schedules. I've been there before; it was happening more frequently for me before the accident. I felt like running was becoming a stressor and I was losing sight of why I did it, instead focusing on just the numbers.

In my experience, when you're so devoted to a rigid plan, that's usually when the unexpected creeps in and slaps you in the face, forcing you to slow down a little and hit the reset button. I've had running injuries before, most of which were very minor in comparison, and although they never required huge amounts of downtime, they were still extremely difficult. I would have a hard time accepting that I needed to slow down. I would resist it and be miserable, obsessing about how much fitness I was losing or how lazy I was being, instead of listening to my body, letting it heal, and engaging my time and energy in something else.

Usually, by the time I had made peace with slowing down and had started to accept and engage with it, that was the time I could return to sport. This process kept me afraid of time off, injury, and slowing down. It encouraged me to stick to my rigid schedule and believe that was the only way to be successful or feel I was doing enough.

The recovery from my accident taught me the importance of slowing down and what that really looks like. It didn't happen overnight, and it took me a while to appreciate the extra time my injuries brought. But that process was vital in helping me find balance.

The quote at the beginning of this chapter is from a good friend of mine, David Steele. Well, David "Powder" Steele, I should say. He gave himself that middle name to avoid confusion with another David Steele in his high school growing up—it doesn't hurt that he's a kick-ass skier. I met David in Montana, at one of my favorite races ever, Run the Rut. He was helping out at the races, marking and sweeping the courses. David was intrigued by the sport of ultrarunning, and on top of that he's just an all-around fun human. His kind, thoughtful, and playful demeanor instantly drew me to him. As we became fast friends, we followed each other's athletic pursuits.

Having dealt with many of his own injuries, David was one of the first to give me clarity from a different perspective. He kept telling me to "honor my process." It looks different for everyone, it will be different for everyone, and it's definitely not all rainbows and unicorns, he told me. But if you honor your process, you will come out the other side stronger, different, and with new knowledge.

At first, I think I missed the point. I thought honoring my process meant honoring my *immediate* process, right now. I needed to be patient with my injuries because I couldn't move or walk in the beginning. I thought this "honoring" should only last about three months, until I could start walking again, and then I'd be fine to continue pushing forward like I always do. But the more I saw how unpredictable and nonlinear my recovery would be, the more I learned the wisdom in David's words.

Honoring my process was a way to honor the change that was about to occur within me. It was a way to accept that I wasn't going to be the same person, and this whole process was about to change not only my whole mentality on sport and being an athlete, but also how I viewed myself. It was just the beginning.

An athlete's biggest Achilles' heel is that our coping mechanism is wound up in the things we do athletically. Our frustrations are only compounded by lack of exercise, so we're in trouble if we can't get rid of them by going on a run or ride or ski. Without exercise as an outlet, the emotions and physical unrest marinate and mix together, creating even more of the same.

This was the process I had to honor every day of my recovery, as well as every day I was healthy. There's always something to battle, something to learn from, and some opportunity to become better. Every low has an important moment in life, to show us what we are made of and offer a chance to cultivate motivation, desire, dreams. Those moments push you through to whatever obstacle comes next. What I had to remember was this: *You are more than just an athlete; keep honoring your process.*

I often wonder how much athletic drive comes from a desire to be good at something because we feel weak or inadequate elsewhere. Is some part of our self-worth bound to being an athlete, on being able to perform? The greatest gift of my injury was learning that performance and accolades were not quite there for me. They were never the motivating factors, and they became a by-product of the process of self-discovery. I had the chance to remember the other parts of myself. It was a reminder to be a whole person.

There is more to life than sport, but when we start to think of life in distinct blocks or chunks of time, little pieces that must fit in exactly the correct space or place in order to feel complete, life can start to feel like a cage. A cage that we are unable to escape even though we set the restrictions and enforce the rules.

Running, which held such a special place in my life and heart, had started to become this trap. I had to complete a certain number of hours of training, run a certain number of miles, or gain a certain number of vertical feet per week for "X" number of weeks in order to feel accomplished. On top of this was the pressure of comparing those numbers to my peers and competitors.

There was a pressure associated with being "elite," one that no longer afforded the luxury of rest, easy days, or adventures. I had to have a purpose for my running. A diligent plan. Going for a run no longer provided enjoyment. It structured my day. I had to go run because I was a runner and I needed to train for my races. I had to run because I feared what would happen if I did not, or what would happen if I simply went out to have fun on the trail with no structure at all. This perception of time, and how running and training fit into that puzzle, began to weigh on me. Running began to lose its magic. It was becoming a game of numbers and time.

During my early ultrarunning career, since I was a pro, I thought I should get a coach. I tried a couple of them, both with impressive running careers and prominent running pedigrees. I, however, did not come from a competitive running background, so I wasn't familiar with structured run training or workouts. I was used to training by feel and doing what I wanted to do that day. If I felt like going hard, I'd go hard up a climb. If I felt like cruising, I'd go slow and look for bugs on the trails, or stop to take pictures.

Since I wasn't accustomed to my time on the trail feeling structured, I struggled early on with the workouts, always doubting my abilities and whether I was going fast enough. I'd stress out the night before and be anxious about the upcoming workout. Again, my perception of time was becoming muddled. Running was morphing into a stressor instead of a pleasure. Something to get over with so I could move on with my day.

If I'm honest with myself, I think I was in the early stages of developing overtraining syndrome (OTS), which is basically the accumulation of multiple stressors, an all-inclusive fatigue that exhausts the mind and body. It's a burnout buildup, but the fatigue is not just due to a training load. The exhaustion stems from multiple factors: not resting, outside stressors, poor diet, poor mental health/dialogue. I don't think I was fully there, but if I had continued down the path I was on, constantly pushing through and telling myself I needed to keep going, it was inevitable. I didn't allow myself to feel tired or to rest. I was a professional now and I needed to perform. If I had continued to put this pressure on myself, training like I was, I think my running could have taken a different turn.

The world of ultrarunning is full of people who are determined high-achievers, and generally type A personalities. In this endurance sport, you *do* need a certain number of hours of training to succeed, but in my opinion you can still find balance—where you're not teetering on the edge of a breakout performance and constant fatigue that leads to injury.

I think elite athletes in the sport realize this fact, but the overarching atmosphere is chock-full of addictive personalities. In my opinion, the balance is easily lost, with athletes conversely encouraged to engage with the "more is better" approach. This can get you in trouble; instead of a culture of encouragement for walking that thin line between overtraining and rest, there's pressure and almost complacent encouragement to go for it and not stop. Ever. Burning both ends of the candle, so to speak, until there's no more candle (i.e. your endocrine system) to burn.

As a young ultrarunner, I was being sucked into this vicious cycle. Thankfully, my path took a different turn and I had the chance to slow down. I was *forced* to slow down. Falling off that cliff forced me into a recovery period, not only physically, but mentally. My body needed a full hard stop to repair itself, and my mind had to be patient. It had to learn to love the sport again, to not take it for granted, to engage with the ups and downs of training and life, and to rediscover the magic of a balanced life.

Those months I spent broken and slowly healing are where I learned the value of time, and the gift that injury can provide. It was then that I started to honor my process. To engage with the other parts of me that made me, me. They were always there, but certain aspects of me became lost or were pushed to the back. I did not give them enough time to be enjoyed or savored.

My injury gave me the chance to discover these things all over again. The joy of reading, of a slow morning sipping extra coffee and staying in bed. The joy of walks, of rich conversations, of connecting with both new and old friends. The joy of teaching and being taught by others. The joy of relationships and the bonds that are built simply by sharing a cooked meal together. I realized there's so much more to this world than the numbers you can record in a training log.

Time began to take on a different pace. It bore the same weight and importance in my mind, but it slowed. I had to focus on one moment at a time, and in doing so, I discovered the beauty of each endeavor. I had the chance to reprioritize my time and decide what I wanted in life. Time was my currency, and I got to decide what I wanted to spend it on.

I learned to honor the process of my recovery and not take for granted the time I had. I got to use it as an opportunity for growth and a reinvestment in what I valued, instead of spending it on things I thought I *should* be doing, simply out of obligation or compulsion.

I also learned this process was far from perfect. There were, and still are, plenty of times I was impatient, unwilling, and stubborn. I didn't want to honor the fact that I was injured and it would take time and patience to recover. I resisted community; I wanted to isolate myself and not burden others, for fear of their pity and judgment. But nothing was worse than the judgment I would pass on myself. So, in time, I learned to let go.

Time away from something is the best way to know if you truly love it, want it, and need it in your life. In my time away from running, I discovered that real connections come from raw vulnerability and opening up in the times I want isolation. I experienced the freedom of a day with no schedule at all, the satisfaction of an honest conversation discussing whatever came to mind, and my curiosity as I observed natural science in the crystallization of water or the ability of insects to camouflage themselves in nature.

It was during this time, this space away from running and competition, that my desire to run and my aspiration to race again began to grow. In this slow period, I got to think about the reasons I run, and the reasons why I wanted to run again. I considered the difference between wanting something and needing it.

Performance is not why I run. Sure, I put pressure on myself, but a finish time or place or result is always a side note and side effect to what I love: running. I don't need to win or compete in order to want to run. They are not dependent on one another. I love the challenge of running, of testing my limits, of proving I can do what I set out to do. I don't necessarily need a competition to do this.

Enjoying the sights, smells, and sounds of nature along the way makes me feel connected to my body, to myself, and to the world around me. It's spiritual for me, my church in a way, and I wouldn't be the same person without the challenges and magnificent experiences of running. It's never been about winning, because the feelings of victory aren't the feelings that last. They are fleeting moments without any gravity. Sometimes I wonder why it took an injury for me to realize this. I still truly felt this way before the injury, but I think I was going through the motions, and it wasn't until I had the space and separation from my passion that I realized how important it was to me, and how lucky I was to run.

Running is a gift. It makes me whole and connected. I feel like I was made to do it. It doesn't define my identity, but it's an integral part of me. This can be a hard line to decipher, but it's how I define the difference between running for the love of it versus running for the podium. This separation is what allowed me to return to running and to competition and, ironically, it's what allowed me to win again.

The start line can be an intimidating place at any time. Even more so after months of doubt, recovery, and running solo, when the whole point is to not compare yourself to others. Returning to a start line with doubts and fears about expectations—wondering if you're the same athlete you once were, wondering if you are still, in fact, elite—is incredibly difficult.

I avoided these thoughts and fears for a long time. I told myself that the year after my accident would be for me, for recovery, and for rediscovery. I didn't want the pressure of racing, of expectation—mostly from myself, but also from the community, which, by the way, was only extremely supportive.

I was afraid. I didn't want to share my running, out of fear that a poor performance would change the way I was viewed or valued in the community or the way I valued myself. I was afraid to compare myself to others, afraid to put myself out there. I secluded myself from the community, instead of immersing myself within it.

Less than a year after my accident, Broken Arrow Skyrace, a race I'd wanted to do for years, began reaching out to me to do their race. I was hesitant, afraid to do it. But I finally signed up and told myself I was only running for fun, not to compete. I even signed up for a vertical kilometer race the day before the main fifty-five-kilometer event. A vertical kilometer (VK) race sounded fun to me; it was a climbing only race in which you climbed 1,000 meters in less than five kilometers.

I wanted to feel a part of the community again, without the pressure, so I signed up for both events and told myself I wouldn't race either of them—I would just do them. For fun. But even that caused anxiety. I was still fearful of a bad result, fearful of judgment, fearful of what my body could or couldn't do. I hadn't run more than twenty miles since the accident, and I doubted what I could handle.

My coach, Adam, said I needed to rip off the Band-Aid. That it didn't matter if I was elite anymore. He told me I needed to do

THE START LINE CAN BE AN INTIMIDATING PLACE AT ANY TIME. EVEN MORE SO AFTER MONTHS OF DOUBT, RECOVERY, AND RUNNING SOLO, WHEN THE WHOLE POINT IS TO NOT COMPARE YOURSELF TO OTHERS.

these races and just run, not for anyone else, but just myself. He wouldn't love me any less or want to stop coaching me, no matter the result. He did offer one bit of odd advice though.

"Race the VK, then just enjoy the ultra," he said. "There's no downhill in that and you're super strong going uphill." I think he knew he needed to get me to that start line. To get my competitive side active.

Getting physically strong enough to complete an ultramarathon after my injuries was no easy feat. The Broken Arrow Skyrace took place only ten months after I fell off that mountain, but I wanted to do it. It seemed like the perfect race, one that encouraged everyone to participate, no matter how fast they went. I liked that ethos, and I wanted to show up for myself and the community that helped me get there.

The hardest part was getting to the start line, acknowledging my fear and embracing it. I remember being calm on the start line of the vertical kilometer race. I knew it was going to hurt. The gun went off, and we sprinted up a grassy hillside. Squaw Valley is at altitude, and within the first 250 meters of the race I had a metallic taste in my mouth. In other words, I tasted blood, I was going that hard. I focused on my breathing. It was labored, but I knew I could hold it. I focused on my stride, putting one foot in front of the other. I let my body do its thing and just kept climbing uphill. It knew how to do that.

I switched from a power hike to a jog, depending on the steepness of the terrain and the metallic taste lingering in my mouth, as if I was sucking on a penny. I was passing people as I climbed. I focused on synchronizing my breath with my footsteps. I tried to smile as I passed familiar faces on the trail. One guy had put a metal goat out on the trail and snapped a picture of it as I ran by. "The Hillygoat!" he screamed. I was enjoying the pain, the effort, the movement.

But as I got to the top of a big hill, I found myself next running downhill. *What?!* I thought to myself. *I thought this was supposed to be a vertical kilometer! Why is there a downhill?* I laughed as I ran downhill as fast as I could. It was only about 500 feet, which I regained quickly as we climbed to the very top of the ski slope at Squaw.

The final section of the course had a metal staircase. As I reached the bottom of it, I saw the first woman topping out. She crossed the finish line as I reached the final stretch, a section of snow stairs lined with flags and photographers. I couldn't help but cross the finish line beaming. I actually had fun out there. I didn't even think about my injured foot or ankles—even on that downhill section! I gave the first-place woman a big hug. She was impressed by my performance. "Every time there was a steep section you were gaining on me!" she said. "I did my best to stay ahead of you!" We were only separated by fifteen seconds in the end. I couldn't believe it. I had impressed myself too. I called my coach as I took the gondola back to center village. Adam just laughed and said, "I knew you'd do well. You're the Hillygoat after all!"

Despite my success and the slight boost in confidence from my result at the vertical kilometer, I was still nervous for the ultra I planned to run the next day. This type of race was what I loved, and I felt like running longer distances was my strength, or at least it used to be. I wasn't sure anymore.

Standing on the start line, my emotions warred in my mind. *Can I do this? Can I complete this race? It's fifty-two kilometers; I haven't run more than forty kilometers in one go. It's a lot of climbing—I can do that—but that means a lot of descending . . . descending still feels bad. Can I do that? Will my foot be OK? Is this a mistake? Should I just go home now? Am I even elite again? What will people think of me? Am I going to come in last and embarrass myself?*

The gun went off.

I started running, thoughts still swirling in my head.

The race was two loops, and the first loop wasn't going smoothly. By kilometer ten I was struggling. I was on the verge of tears and trying to hold them back. The first part of the course was a runnable uphill, and I still didn't feel strong on this type of terrain. Other runners were passing me, and I felt sorry for myself. Then came the steep, loose descents and I found myself braking out of fear, upset with myself.

I kept telling myself it was OK. I was running for me, not them. I'd stop crying for a few minutes, and then run through the aid station with people cheering my name and telling me how strong I was. Then I'd start crying all over again. I didn't feel strong. I was hurting and broken, and my mind felt stuck.

I neared the high point of the course with "emotional intervals," crying intermittently as I made my way up the hill. Near the top of the climb was a ladder and a slightly exposed section. It was right here that I saw Martina Valmassoi, one of the photographers on the ridge who was with me on the mountainside the day of my fall. She was snapping photos and yelling words of encouragement. At the sight of her, my crying intensified. I stopped running and gave her a big hug.

She ran with me a little bit, telling me how proud she was of me and that she'd see me on the next lap.

"I'm doing so bad," I told her.

"Fuck what other people say, Hillary," she said. "You are doing great. You are so strong to even be here."

As I wiped my tears away and made my way down the first descent, I knew I was going to finish. I hugged some friends at the halfway-point aid station, and as I began my second lap, my concentration and strength grew. I started to believe in myself. I began passing people, encouraging them as I went. I didn't care what place I got or what it looked like. I wanted to get to that finish line and celebrate my journey of getting back to running in the mountains.

On this lap, I smiled, I laughed, and I enjoyed the community around me. I even enjoyed the downhill and tried to push a little bit. I felt the freedom of running, and for brief instances, I didn't remember I was injured or "coming back" from something. I was just me, enjoying the movement and being free with my own two feet.

As I crossed the finish line, body still intact, feeling good and surrounded by my running family, I broke down into tears again. This time, happy ones. I hugged the race directors and my friends, so grateful for the experience and the welcoming community. I still wasn't sure if I was elite anymore, but just showing up to that start line and trying, despite the promise of a result, was what made it all worth it. Running was mine again, and I was doing it for the joy and the pleasure of it. I was happy. I was fulfilled. This wasn't a comeback. It was something different entirely, something sweeter, more unique and distinctive. I was on a new path, able to decipher my own goals and meaning, regardless of a result or podium finish.

I left that run feeling more complete and whole and able to take on new challenges—accepting the fear and unknown, but choosing to go for it anyway. I didn't know that embracing this mindset would allow me to return to the top of my sport again. But letting go of expectation and doing something I loved just because I love it allowed me, ironically, to win again.

A week after my return to racing at the vertical kilometer race and Broken Arrow Skyrace, I traveled to one of my favorite places on earth: Cortina d'Ampezzo, in the Dolomites of Italy. The North Face was a title sponsor for this race, and I was going to support the team and give a talk.

It wasn't until Wednesday of that week that I decided I wanted to race too. I signed up for the Cortina Trail forty-eight-kilometer race and was on the start line that Saturday. I didn't know what would happen, or if I was recovered from my races the previous weekend, but I didn't care. I just wanted to run. I wanted the freedom I had just experienced the weekend before in Squaw Valley. I wanted to be on those beautiful trails in the Dolomites, enjoying their sweeping, rugged beauty. I wanted to run across the crumbling calcium carbonate that looked like snow from afar. I wanted to feel the burn in my lungs, to forget about my fears and doubts about running or being elite again. I wanted to run for the sake of running, the enjoyment, and the inevitable ecstasy that would ensue.

As I stood in the center of Cortina, gazing across the valley floor, memories flooded back to me. Memories of a time before the accident . . . my first trip here to the Dolomites, winning this race, smiling, happy, completely unaware of the journey ahead. Now I stood in the same place, in front of the turquoise church in the center of town, watching the race volunteers construct the start/ finish line arch. A huge rush of warmth flowed over my body, filling my eyes with tears and warming my cheeks. I was here, against all odds. I had proven those doctors wrong. I had run. I was running. I was competing. I hadn't given up, and I wasn't about to now.

I stepped into the starting corral as the race announcer introduced me and asked me a couple of questions. "Hillary, you've been to Cortina before, yes?" he asked in a thick Italian accent. "You are defending your win here two years ago. How do you feel?"

I smiled. "I'm really happy to be here and enjoy a beautiful day." I took a few strides out of the starting gate, jumping up and down as I gazed across the blue horizon. The sun was already hot on my skin. I took a sip of water out of my flask as the announcer began to count down the race start. "Ten, nine, eight . . ."

I took a deep breath, bouncing up and down as I poised my finger to start my watch. *Enjoy it, Hill. Enjoy every step. It's a gift.*

Bang! At the sound of the gun, everything else turned silent. I could only hear the sound of my breathing as I set my gaze up the winding road to the single track ahead.

As I reached the trail, already 500 feet above the city center, my heart felt full and happy. I was smiling. My legs felt fluid and strong, flowing easily on the uphill. I remembered the trails, the views, the feeling of running, of competing. I was fully immersed. I ran through river crossings, smiled through aid stations. My North Face teammates cheered for me as I reached the aid stations. I was enjoying the race so much. Every climb fed my soul as I settled into my stride and ticked away each vertical foot. On the descents, I felt timid at first, but I gained confidence with each one—and soon enough, I felt like I was flying.

I didn't even know what place I was in until I reached the city center of Cortina and saw them place the finish tape across the finish line. I won the race, only five minutes off the course record. I had done it. I had won a race! I wasn't "back." I hadn't had a "comeback." I was better, improved, and new. I was different. A new kind of athlete—one whose happiness and self-worth doesn't require winning, one whose self-confidence and joy brought out the best results. I was a new kind of athlete – one with that sweater gifted to me from Matt, my PT at Revo, to remind me of how far I'd come.

Later that year I did another race, an eighty-kilometer race (fifty miles) in the foothills of the Andes Mountains outside Santiago, Chile. I won that race too, proving to myself that I was capable of running ultras once again, not because I was fully recovered physically, but because I was happy again—mentally and emotionally fulfilled. In fact, after my injury, I did some of the biggest training weeks I have ever done in my athletic career—completing the Hardrock 100 Course in three days (the "Softrock"), running my first stage race at the TransRockies Run, and doing my own "soft" UTMB (Ultra-Trail du Mont Blanc, a 105-mile course around Mount Blanc crossing through France, Italy, and Switzerland) in four days for my thirtieth birthday.

I was happy, and because of that I was healthy and able to do things in training that I had never even considered before.

Honoring my process brought me to this. If I hadn't been forced to face my injuries and recovery, I don't think I would have discovered this.

And it's never over. I'm still constantly learning, constantly honoring my process. Being an athlete and a human being isn't a math equation. It's not solely a numbers game, regarding paces or time spent training. It's more complex and beautiful than that. There are many ups and downs, highs and lows, moments when you want to quit and moments when you feel invincible. Each of these is a part of the process, and honoring each piece is what makes the whole picture come together.

I still struggle. I still have hard days. I still have to acknowledge the fear I feel on a start line or leading up to a race, or sometimes even before a workout—fear that a bad performance will cause others to dislike me, or my coach to think I'm weak, or me to dislike myself. Fear that not living up to expectations (mostly my own) will lead to a life as an outcast. And that's OK. It's OK to have these fears, to recognize them, work through them, and honor them, while not allowing them to take root. To embrace the fear and move through it. I think that's what my friend David meant when he kept telling me to *honor my process*. It looks different for everyone, and each moment is worth honoring and working through. For me, honoring the lows along with the highs is what allowed me to reach a new level of self-acceptance, athletic performance, and authentic joy.

9 WAY OF THE WARRIOR

One of the first pairs of running shoes I had was the La Sportiva Bushido. I liked them because they felt sturdy, with lots of lateral stabilization, like the shoes I wore when I played tennis in college. I felt fast, able to dodge any rock on the trail. When I slipped those shoes on, I could tackle anything: mud, roots, and my favorite steep mountain terrain. I ran many miles in those shoes. I could rely on them, I trusted them, I felt fast in them. They quickly became a favorite, and the more I wore them in, the more comfortable they became.

I ran those shoes into the ground, unwilling to part ways with them, even when my feet started to hurt after all the miles I had traveled with them. They were worn out. We had traveled long distances together, over numerous mountain passes and through lots of adventures, and I didn't want to give them up. I felt a closeness with these shoes, loyalty. I told myself I would get a new pair. I even tried some on. But the newer model of the shoe felt so different that I no longer liked it. They didn't hug my feet or make me feel ready to tackle anything.

So, I kept that old pair of Bushidos, tucked away in my closet, wearing them occasionally for short runs, loving the feel of them, not letting go. One day, when I was spring cleaning, I found them at the back of my closet. I thought about tossing them, but instead my curious nature kicked in. I had always liked the name. *Bushido.* But I never knew what it actually meant. It didn't seem like an Italian name, although the brand La Sportiva is Italian. I didn't know what "Bushido" had to do with Italy.

My questions led me to learn that *bushido* is the collective term for "way of the Samurai" in Japanese. It literally means "the way of the warrior." I couldn't get rid of these shoes! They were my armor. I tucked them safely in the back of my closet, where they would be ready for me the next time I might need them, or simply a reminder of how to be a warrior.

The way of the warrior, for me, is like recovery. And like recovery, it's really a way of life. All-encompassing. It's a state of mind. It's fluid in its inclusion of all things. There's no separation between you and the warrior, between you and recovery, between you and forward progression. The way of the warrior is a path, a way of living. You can't give up on it, because it's part of you, so therefore, by default, you are 100 percent all in.

When I was faced with my recovery, this wasn't a passive decision. Of course, I had to slow down and give my body time to heal. Choosing the way of the warrior was more an active choice to *participate* in recovery—not just let it happen to me. This was a skill I was unaware I possessed.

Of course, I'm no good at sitting around and waiting, biding my time, hoping things will be better. Instead, I became an active participant, and my best recovery was accomplished this way, as I worked through the discomfort.

The path for me meant accepting every mental block, setback, and feeling of entrapment within my body and working through it all. I refused to give up and instead chose to find the way through.

There were times—frequently, if I'm being honest—when I didn't want to show up to a warehouse for physical therapy, stuck inside doing the same routine under fluorescent lights every day. It was taxing, exhausting, uninspiring. But on every one of those mornings, when my motivation was waning, I would think about the path I was on—the one of a warrior fighting her way back to what she wanted, fighting for what she believed she could do. The warrior mentality was in me, somewhere, and if I held on to it, I knew I'd find a way through.

I don't believe in shortcuts. If I want something, I work to get it, taking the hard way—the uphill-both-ways version. That's all I know how to do. So, when I hear of people, or runners, looking for a quick fix to overcome injury, depression, obstacles, you name it, I truly don't understand. I believe that if you really want something, you must commit yourself to finding a way through the muck. This is what drives me when things get difficult. It's at my core.

Some might describe it as obsessive, and automatically put a negative spin on it, assuming that it brings out the worst in me. But I disagree. My tenacity and determination are gifts and strengths, and they became tools, not just in my recovery, but in other aspects of my life.

When those doctors told me I would never compete or run again, I knew, right then, I had a choice. I could give up and give in, accepting what they thought was inevitable, normal or, expected, or I could fight and battle. I could face my fear right in the eye. I could look deep within myself and embrace the pain, the struggle, and the unknown. In doing so, I held the power to dictate my fate. Not the doctors. I chose to work hard every day, relentlessly, to determine what was possible for myself.

This determination is my bushido. It's my "way of the warrior." It's palpable, a fierceness I possess, a beautiful stubbornness and unwillingness to give up. But it's not always easy to manage. In fact, it's forced me to choose myself over friendships or relationships. It's left me questioning whether my love for running, travel, and independence and my strong opinions are too much for societal norms. It's left me wondering if I need to change those parts of me in order to be accepted or categorized in a "normal" way.

From the time I was young, I've always had these qualities. As a child, it was just who I was. I didn't question it; it was just me. I embraced it. My mother recognized it too, and when my stubbornness surfaced, she would often laugh, knowing this was the daughter she was raising—feistiness and all.

I've heard the legendary stories of my childhood that demonstrate my spirit. There was the time I wanted my mother's attention, but she was busy. So I stood on the doorstep, hands on my hips, with a perturbed scowl on my face, eyes locked on my mother's, and . . . peed. Yes, that's right. I peed on the floor. Then I turned and strutted away. I must have been five years old. All my mother could do was laugh and shake her head.

Once I mistakenly went skiing with two left boots. Cross-country skiing was a favorite family activity during the Colorado winters. We would drive up the Poudre Canyon to our favorite summer trails, strap on our skis, and tour for hours around the frozen landscape.

The day before skiing we went to rent our gear from our local ski shop. My feet were growing like weeds, and I needed different boots every year. The next day we loaded up all our gear and headed out on the hour-and-a-half drive to a beautiful trailhead that paralleled a river leading deep into the canyon.

We layered up and began getting our things together: snacks, water, gloves, hats, boots, and skis. But when I went to put my boots on, one didn't feel quite right. As we took a closer look, we realized the ski shop had mixed up my boots and I was stuck with two left boots.

Dad was infuriated, as was my mother. But I was only disappointed. I really wanted to ski. We had driven all the way up the canyon. Barkely, our yellow lab, was already frolicking in the snow. My sister was skating around the parking lot, oblivious to the problem, enjoying the movement of her skis over the snow. Meanwhile, my parents were trying to figure out the problem.

"Glenda, what are we going to do? Can we go back?" Dad questioned, his voice tinged with annoyance and disappointment. But I didn't want to go back.

"I want to try to ski for a little bit," I told them, "to see how it feels." We were there anyway. I promised to tell them if my foot hurt too much, and we would head back. But I knew I wouldn't be turning back. I was as determined as ever to enjoy skiing.

My foot hurt from the first kick, glide, and push of my ski, but I didn't say a word. I was too focused on the snow and the fun I was having. We skied for four hours. My right foot was sore for a couple of days after, but it was completely worth it.

As I got older, that tenacity and determination translated to my schoolwork, athletics, and hobbies. I didn't think there was anything I couldn't do. If I wanted something, I found a way to make it happen.

I learned to play tennis in ninth grade. I loved it. The strategy, the athleticism, the tactical momentum ... I devoted myself to the sport so much that by my senior year I had earned a scholarship to play tennis in college. In college, everything was on another level. The team had its own private courts, reserved for whenever we wanted to play. I even got a key to the racket center so I could hit balls on the ball machine after classes.

I was majoring in chemistry, so my class load was fairly heavy. I was busy. I was focused. Aside from my studies and playing tennis, I also served on the student body government, and had jobs as a tutor and a tour guide for the admissions office.

I was hardworking and committed to every activity, and I was happy about it. But most people my age didn't understand me. My teammates gave me a hard time, telling me to loosen up and have more fun. I was confused. I *was* having fun. I was fulfilled. I was enjoying the grind and ticking off what I needed to do each day to achieve my goals. I liked being so involved and having a sense of purpose. I saw it as pieces of a bigger picture, and I was trying to absorb and learn as much as I could to take with me into the rest of my life.

Of course, my peers' version of fun involved the typical party lifestyle that college advertises and enables. And eventually, peer pressure and its gravitational force wore me down, so I decided to attend a party and "loosen up."

Some of my tennis teammates had organized the party, and it was my first. I didn't quite know what to expect. I only felt that I needed to attend to prove to my teammates and friends that I could have fun—their kind of fun—and lighten up and make friends. So, I went.

As I walked in, it was like a scene from a movie unfolding in real time right in front of me. Country music was blaring (and I hate country music) as my friends and teammates were laughing, drinking, and yelling over a game of beer pong. I had never played before and didn't know what to do. My teammate Lindsay came to greet me, draping me in a big hug. I could smell the sweetness of alcohol and perfume all over her. She was giggly and happy, escorting me into the kitchen, where there was an enormous amount of alcohol. Maybe fifteen different bottles of liquor. She asked me what I wanted, listing everything they had. "Or maybe you want a beer," she said as she opened the fridge, which was overflowing with various six-packs. I felt completely overwhelmed. I wanted so desperately to fit in, but I felt so out of my skin. I smiled at Lindsay, grabbed a beer I recognized from the fridge, and made my way out of the kitchen, timidly sipping the drink and searching for a familiar face in the room.

I BELIEVE THAT IF YOU REALLY WANT SOMETHING, YOU MUST COMMIT YOURSELF TO FINDING A WAY THROUGH THE MUCK. THIS IS WHAT DRIVES ME WHEN THINGS GET DIFFICULT. IT'S AT MY CORE.

I am friendly and outgoing, so I relied on that, talking to everyone I knew, being sociable, smiling, laughing. Anyone who saw me at this party would have thought I was having a good time, and my teammates were happy I was there. But I felt uncomfortable. I wasn't relaxed and I certainly wasn't having fun. I was counting down the minutes until I could leave. I was bored by the conversations and felt like I had nothing to contribute to the theme of "What's the stupidest thing you've done while drunk?" I had never been drunk. I felt ashamed to admit that, so I laughed at the stories, hoping they wouldn't look to me to tell one of my own. All I wanted to do was go home.

As the laughter and stories swirled around me, I was making a list in my mind of the things I had to do the next day: get up early to practice at the racket center, study for my exams, do all my homework, and go grocery shopping. But, despite my distraction and dissatisfaction, I continued to stay, sipping the same lukewarm beer so no one would question why I wasn't drinking or pressure me to get another drink if they saw my hands empty.

I kept thinking to myself, *Hillary, if you're not having any fun, then why are you staying? You can leave whenever you want . . . just say goodbye and walk out the door.* But I stayed. I stayed as everyone continued to get more drunk and belligerent, and the conversations disintegrated into incoherent babbling. I stayed because I was trying to fit in. I was trying to prove to my teammates and friends that I was "fun" and "normal"—or at least that I could fit their definition of "normal." But it was only myself I was betraying. I was ignoring who I was, at my core. I couldn't bear the feeling any longer. Finally, I turned to my doubles partner, Kati. "I have to go to the bathroom," I announced. "Can you watch this for me?" I pointed to my beer on the table as I got up to weave my way through the crowd. I walked right past the bathroom in the hallway and straight out the front door.

Attending that party was the first moment I doubted myself and my focused determination. I let other people's opinions get into my head, making me want to change a part of me, the aspects of myself that gave me purpose, direction, and dedication. For the first time, I felt like I needed to be a different version of myself in order to fit in. But the uneasy feeling coursing through me at that party, the one I couldn't bear because I was betraying myself, convinced me that I couldn't pretend. I couldn't hide from who I was.

From then on, I told myself if I wanted to attend parties, I could. And I would, but I would do it my way. The Hillary way. Parties happened with a plan, so I could feel engaged with my friends, but still true to myself. I would go, talk with my friends, play a few games, and have a few laughs. But by 9 p.m. I would "go to the bathroom" and make my escape for home, where I could unwind the way I liked: drink some tea, make a plan for the next day, have some alone time, and get to bed so I would wake rested and ready to seize my day the next morning.

This made me happy, and I was unwilling to compromise my happiness for the sake of fitting in. I couldn't sacrifice who I was for anyone else. I had to follow who I was, and I decided to love those stubborn, determined, goal-driven parts of me and not let "popular" opinion get in the way of it.

It's not always easy to ignore peer pressure or go against the grain. As a woman who possesses more masculine characteristics, this was especially true throughout my young adult life—my fierce independence, strong opinions, and need for solitude have been social obstacles to finding real relationships and friendships.

I have often chosen my personal goals, instead of sacrificing them for a significant other. This isn't a quality that's encouraged for women. Women are expected to be agreeable and neutral, to not take up too much space or draw too much unwanted attention, to not have too many opinions or to speak them too loudly.

But these subdued qualities are not ones I possess, and I have been criticized for them, questioned, and ridiculed. Told that I would end up alone and lonely, unless I conformed.

In certain moments, for just a split second, I might start to doubt my decision to stick to my passions, follow my dreams, and state my opinions. I might start to believe it was true, that I would wind up alone or alienate myself, that I was too difficult, too driven, too goal-oriented, and too opinionated. I might start to think that I must change these things about myself in order to be loved and accepted.

But those doubts and feelings were always fleeting. Deep down in my gut, I have never viewed my traits as a disadvantage. And every decision I made to support myself and go after my dreams—including leaving behind the potential for a "comfortable" life—I viewed as opportunities, not misfortunes. In fact, in my opinion, the bigger failure would have been to deny who I truly am, or what I knew I wanted and couldn't do if I chose to compromise myself or my dreams for someone else's.

So, I've always stuck to my beliefs and my core values, trusting that I would draw upon a community that truly understood me and wouldn't ask or demand anything of me that I couldn't provide. I chose to be patient, and somewhere along the line, that's exactly what happened.

Sticking to who I was, and not allowing outside noise or pressure to dictate my life decisions and choices, allowed me to discover running and a community of people involved with running. In this community I could be tenacious, persistent, stubborn, and determined with my goals and how I pursued them. I felt supported and celebrated for my spirit and who I was. No one asked me to change or be anything but myself. Running allowed me to rediscover—and celebrate—my strengths.

Showing up for what you believe in and who you are is import-ant. I am different from other people, and I can't shed what makes me different. I refuse to change. It's like the *bushido,* the way of the warrior. It's a part of me, of who I am. It's not always the easi-est path, but in the end, I find it's one that's always worth it.

Embracing the way of the warrior has permanence; it's not changeable. When the warrior puts down her sword after the bat-tle, it's not the end of her fight. She might put the armor to rest, at the back of the closet in a safe space, but it's ready for when the time comes again to go into battle. Of course, you hope the next time never comes, but that part of you, the warrior, is never dead or gone.

I learned this lesson seventeen months into my recovery. After battling the odds, returning to form, racing, and winning several races, I was ready for a full race season. I was excited to tackle some exciting races and new challenges. I felt healthy, and for the first time since my initial injuries I felt normal—not like an injured runner, but myself, strong and physically capable of any challenge.

I woke up one morning in late January to fresh snow. We had been having a lot of snowstorms that winter in Boulder. It was a good snow year. I didn't have plans to ski this particular morning, so I decided to get out for a run—I love running in fresh snow. I made plans to run on Mount Sanitas, knowing that the snow was coming down heavy and the bigger mountains on the front range would already have deep snow accumulation. I didn't want it to be a slog, so I decided to stay shorter and lower. The trail was *covered* in deep snow. I hiked up the steep ridge to the top of the moun-tain, catching snowflakes on my tongue and in my eyelashes. It was cold, maybe 15 degrees Fahrenheit. I could see my breath as I exhaled with each stride.

After reaching the top of the mountain I started down the back side to the smooth valley trail. I could see the entire skyline of

Boulder, with its flatirons covered in snow. It felt like I was in a winter wonderland. As the trail ended, I made my way back home, zigzagging my way through the neighborhood. Cars had already been out and packed down the snow in spots. When I turned onto Mariposa Avenue, only four blocks from home, I felt my foot slip out from under me, and my ankle twisted to compensate. As my right ankle twisted, so did my body. I heard a pop and crumbled to the cold, snowy ground.

I screamed inside my head. I knew what had just happened. I had broken my ankle. I scooted my way to the sidewalk and tried to stand up. I couldn't. I started to sob. All I could think was, *I don't know if I can do this again.*

After a week of grieving and feeling sorry for myself, I visited the back of my closet. I found my warrior armor, and that feeling of power came back to me again: the way of the warrior. I started to cultivate my warrior mentality, realizing I'd had it all along. I'd had the way of the warrior all my life; it was already within me. I just needed to use it again. It was time to put on the armor, go to the back of my closet, find those Bushidos, lace them up, embrace the process, and go into battle once again.

WHEN YOU EAT DIRT

I can never get enough of something I love. Even when I eat dirt and I'm on the ground suffering, it's fleeting. The misery never compares to the freedom to explore when outside. I've always been that way.

I started camping before I could walk. My mother carried me in a BabyBjörn, facing outward, legs dangling. As a baby, I wanted to see everything, touch everything, and put everything in my mouth. My hands were permanently outstretched, reaching for pinecones, dirt, or worms, my eyes big and wide with curious anticipation. I was always smiling as a kid. Always curious. Especially when my mother would sit me down and let me play in the dirt.

On one camping trip in the Rocky Mountains of Colorado, we had gathered around the picnic table after a hike. I couldn't walk yet, so I was cozy against my mother's chest as she prepared lunch for my dad and my older sister. We were making the rounds, setting out plastic silverware, lunch meat, and fruit on the table. I was grabbing for food as much as I could, stuffing what my mom would allow into my face. But the picnic table was placed rather precariously, and my mom tripped.

Down she went, face-first toward the ground, arms outstretched. But it was my face that broke her fall. She frantically scrambled up to wipe the dirt from my tear-streaked face and mouth and eyes. There was dirt in my teeth and cuts on my cheeks. But before long, I was smiling again, sitting at the picnic table and eating my lunch—mixed with a little dirt.

I slept hard that night, worrying my mother. She kept prying my eyes open every couple of hours to make sure I was alive, worried I was injured or had a concussion. But I was fine. And the next day, I was back to normal, bouncing around in the BabyBjörn, legs dangling, arms outstretched, and eyes roaming everywhere—there was no evidence of my face-plant in the dirt, except for a few fresh cuts on my face.

That's how running has fit into my life—and so have the setbacks. Any time I fall, I'm determined to get back up and keep moving. Sure, I don't want to eat dirt. It doesn't taste that good, and it lingers in your mouth long after you think you're rid of it, gritting between your teeth and clogging up taste buds. (Apparently, I've eaten a lot of dirt; otherwise, I wouldn't know this.) But I'll take a little bit of dirt every now and then if it gives me appreciation for the course, the struggle, and the good when it comes around.

I have to admit, though: sometimes I get sick of constantly having to learn the hard way and be the one who's different. I've been different my whole life, and sometimes I tire of being the one who sticks out or speaks up.

When I played tennis in college, it was fun, and I worked hard, but as I said before, I never really fit in with the team. I was more of a tomboy, and my teammates were girly girls, cliquey and sometimes downright mean. These women were competitive about looks, style, and who could be the skinniest by spring break. I'm not kidding. There was actually a contest a senior tennis player had with her girlfriends, to see who could lose the most weight by bikini season. I ignored this at first, never giving my body a second thought. My body was strong, great at playing tennis. I felt confident. I didn't need to change anything.

But this type of negative energy weighs on a person, and by my junior year of college I had developed an eating disorder and was becoming shockingly thin. My tennis game suffered, while my relationship with my teammates flourished. I was accepted, understood. I, too, was part of their self-deprecating, low-self-esteem club. The experience was mentally taxing. I was shocked by how quickly my confidence disappeared, and I relied on external validation to be accepted, to feel loved or worthy.

Staring into the mirror one day, I didn't recognize the person in front of me. The face reflecting back held no life or vibrancy. My mind was constantly riddled with thoughts of restriction, criticism, deprivation, and self-loathing. Unless I acted fast, I knew I would lose who I was. That was not a path I wanted to go down. But I knew I couldn't do it alone. Sucked deep into this mess, I needed help to see clearly, to find myself again. Over Christmas, I took an extended break of six weeks and checked myself into a treatment facility.

Every day I went to a treatment clinic all day and attended meetings, therapy sessions, and group therapy sessions. I ate all my meals there and went to my apartment on the campus of the clinic at the end of the day.

Learning about myself again—and why I was doing this to myself and why I wanted to stop—was intense. Over the weeks I began to identify appropriate coping mechanisms to deal with my emotions and feelings of inadequacy. I grew to not be afraid of feeling full. To accept myself for my imperfections and give myself a break from the internal pressures I put on myself. I began to become familiar with my emotions, and instead of pushing them aside or numbing them with food—or lack thereof—I began to engage with them, to process them and really feel their breadth and depth. In a way, I was becoming an adult. Learning how to be a fully formed human being with imperfections, ugly and beautiful all at once. I was learning to be my authentic self.

Even after the extensive therapy, when I returned to my senior year of college, I continued to see a therapist on a weekly basis. I enjoyed the talk therapy, and it helped me sort my emotions, as did journaling. I was finding my voice and my stride again. I was in recovery from my eating disorder, and with hard work and dedication I let myself call myself "recovered" from my eating disorder.

Nevertheless, habits die hard, and for many who suffer from anorexia or bulimia, even when they are recovered it's not something that just goes away, never to return again. Sometimes the thoughts creep back in. There were times when I thought about going down that path again, or even had small relapses. I wasn't perfect. It took time, patience, and forgiveness. This was part of me now, and I had to give myself the room to work through it. I had the perspective to know I didn't want to return to a path that wasn't good for me in the long run. I stayed recovered from my eating disorder, and one of the main motivations for me was when I found trail running.

I think trail running saved me. I started running in a healthy way, not an obsessive manner or as a way to punish myself or stay thin. I started running because I truly loved it. It made me feel alive. When I was running, it didn't matter what I looked like. I just listened to how my body felt. And it felt strong and powerful, like it belonged there. The more I ran, the hungrier I got, and I knew that I couldn't trail run how I wanted to if I didn't fuel my body. I also knew I needed muscles to get up the steep mountain terrain that I loved. An eating disorder didn't make sense. There was no room for it. I had to fuel my body and trust that it would tell me what it needed so I could keep doing what I loved. And my body was right. The more I trained, the more I ate. Nutritious, healthy, good food. My relationship with my body, food, and exercise completely changed. There was balance, and I had never felt healthier or happier.

Over the years, and especially as my professional athletic career developed, I worked hard to keep that relationship a priority in my life, and not let someone else's perception of beauty skew my own or cause me to doubt my strengths and performances at my weight. I didn't need to be rail-thin to run. My body knew what to do.

But as soon as I started competing, that eating disorder voice grew louder. I kept seeing these stick-thin runners and wondered, *Do I need to look like that to run? Do I need to lose weight to run faster?*

I'd have mini-meltdowns and call my coach or therapist, both of whom would set my thoughts straight and help me find my way again and ignore the noise. But I was tired of the feeling. Why was I always the one who had to be different, who had to show others there wasn't just one way to do something? It was exhausting! I felt like every time I made progress, or gained momentum, I would fall and find myself eating dirt all over again. So I shouldn't have been surprised that, when I felt my strongest, I was blindsided.

June 4, 2016. Ultra Skyrunning Madeira in Madeira, Portugal. I only had 5.5 kilometers left, all downhill. *Focus for thirty more minutes*, I told myself. Extra time never hurt. The course was brutal—a fifty-five-kilometer race boasting 4,000 meters (13,000 feet) of gain. Technical, steep, hot—just what I liked. It was a very competitive race, and I had pushed into second place.

As I rounded the final corner to push up the last hill, I finally let myself feel the victory as chills ran over my body. There was excitement, relief, accomplishment, and the need for more water—and to take off my shoes. When I crossed the finish, I had made the podium—and fought for every single second of it. I was proud, happy to be done, and pleased with my strength and patience throughout the race.

I hung out at the finish line, congratulating other racers as they came in, drinking water and stretching. Soon I would go back to my hotel to shower and eat something before the athletes and volunteers gathered to share congratulations over dinner. It was always great to celebrate. We would relive the race, telling stories of our ups and downs, the views, the terrain, and our feelings, assuring the organizers they had put on a really tough race.

Everyone kept telling me how strong I was, how hard I pushed on the uphills, that I was a machine. They were impressed, and I was proud of my effort. Then one of the local runners had a surprising question for me.

"How much do you weigh?" he asked, openly comparing me to Gemma Arenas Alcázar, the race winner, who was standing right next to me. About five feet tall, Gemma was petite. Not only was I nine inches taller than Gemma, we had completely different builds. I was the more muscular of the two.

I immediately blushed, my mind racing to navigate an answer. Then came the follow-up question, addressing what he was really getting at. "How is it you can run so fast when you weigh so much . . . more?"

Strength. Machine. Powerful. An animal.

Those were the adjectives others had used to describe me as we celebrated the end of the race. Not fast, or skilled, or talented, or even "runner." I couldn't help but wonder: was it because of the way I looked?

I also couldn't help but be slightly offended, hurt, and extremely self-conscious by the questions of this man—one whom I had beaten by over an hour in the race. I had just finished second, in a world-class competition. Now someone was asking me to explain my performance, as if it were a fluke.

Immediately, my first thoughts were, *Why am I here? How did I run that fast? It must be a mistake; I don't look like I'm supposed to.* I let those thoughts get pretty loud inside my head. I focused on the comments of others, on the doubts they raised. I let them interfere with the celebration of my achievement. That night I let myself stagger down a negative spiral of confusion and self-deprecation, crying and wishing I could change how I looked to avoid future speculation, both from others and my own critical eye.

When I started running, that was when I decided to take care of myself, to listen to my body and respect it. Although I am recovered now, it's a dynamic process, and one I can never ignore. That fact was made clear by the sheer devastation prompted by a single comment about my weight.

But today, in my newfound ability to take a moment to think and separate my thoughts from destructive actions, I choose to challenge doubt and fear. Moving forward from that race, I decided to pick myself up, wipe the dirt from my face, and take on the challenge in front of me.

I don't need to look different to be considered a runner. I am one. I challenge that thought, in all of us. Take a breath, and decide to take action. Maybe that action is an out-loud declaration. Maybe it's quiet introspection or venting. For me, it's sometimes an all-out battle in my head to accept the uncomfortable thoughts urging me, convincing me that I don't "look like a runner," the thoughts compelling me to change my physical state to match an accepted standard. To make myself smaller, to fit inside boundaries or within certain borders.

These standards are bullshit. Complete. Total. Irrational. Bullshit. I've never been one to fit any standard. So why would I start now?

I can run. I can move. Uphill.

Strong. Fast. Running.

I *am* a runner.

What is a runner "supposed" to look like, anyway? Do I run? If so, then I am a runner, no matter the size and shape of my body, no matter the distance covered, or the terrain encountered. Being a runner is simply running.

I was made to run. My soul feels it, my body knows it, my heart longs for it. These are the thoughts I choose to listen to. Not the ones associated with a standard of beauty, strength, or speed. I am a runner just as I am. I choose to run toward that truth.

When did it become acceptable for eating to be shameful? For an athlete to be criticized for her appearance, rather than applauded for her accomplishments? When did it become OK to starve yourself after a workout, instead of nourishing and replenishing yourself, to feel full and happy? When did it become OK for women to celebrate losing their periods because they've trained so hard, or to become so rail-thin that a hard training week might push them over the edge into chronic fatigue or cause a stress fracture? When did a standard for beauty become the equation to success for an athlete? When did the number of abs or ribs you can see indicate your finishing time or if you are more likely to get a podium spot? These are questions I ask myself to deliver perspective. To be in touch with reality.

These questions remind me these standards and pressures are unrealistic, not to mention unhealthy. I don't stand for them, nor do I believe in them. I know that I'm at my healthiest and happiest when I fuel myself in the most nutritious way I can. I run my fastest when I'm carrying muscle and enough fat to have my period, even during the most intense training cycles.

But it isn't easy to be different or criticized. It's uncomfortable and frustrating to be constantly ridiculed and scrutinized against these intangible, impossible standards. And no matter how independent, stubborn, and self-reliant I am, I still feel discouraged that I'm constantly fighting these battles, both outwardly and inwardly. But one thing that frees me from that battlefield is knowing that my strength and athletic build helped save my life during my accident.

I wasn't a bag of bones bouncing down those rocks, and I believe the physical strength of my body is not only what protected me from completely breaking and dying from that fall, but also what sustained my recovery.

Some might think my recovery was quick or amazing, remarkable even. But it was a lot of hard work, a lot of dedication, a lot of trust in my own body to let it heal itself—and a lot of intention to listen to my body. To fuel it properly during the healing process and to celebrate that it was strong enough to heal because I wasn't malnourished or deprived of essential nutrition. My physical strength—despite my body being constantly ridiculed, critiqued for not being thin enough, compared to an ideal standard of fitness or "thinness" to determine its worth—is the very thing that saved my life and my running career. After my injury, I uncovered what real strength looks like. What real strength feels like, deep down at the core. I wouldn't trade that for anything.

Even with my newfound acceptance and confidence—taking the path less traveled and finding ways to ignore outward scrutiny, defining success and worth on my own terms—life is never short on challenges to truly test my character.

I made a full recovery and started racing after all of my injuries, but I spent a year and a half feeling inadequate and injured, lacking confidence in my ability to commit to a full season. When I finally, at the beginning of 2019, felt ready, I was excited about the year, about racing, and about my race calendar. For the first time since the accident, I didn't feel like an injured or recovering runner. I was dreaming again. Creating a race season. Choosing races that excited me, challenged me, and scared me. I felt confident and ready to start my season.

Coming off ski season, January 1 marked the start of my training for the next year. For the first time since my injuries, I was ready to do structured workouts. I felt strong. I felt motivated. It all seemed to be coming together. I felt like this was the year I could celebrate all of the hard work I had done in getting back to where I wanted to be.

But, just like that fateful day in Norway, everything changed with one step. That last week of January was when I slipped on a snowy road and broke my ankle. In a split second I crumbled from confident and ready to embrace the racing season to a sobbing, broken heap on the frozen ground, a mere four blocks from home.

As a friend took me to see the doctor, I sat huddled in the front seat, an emotional wreck. I felt like another war was beginning, when I had just finished fighting the first. As we drove to the doctor's office, my sobs were uncontrollable, the hyperventilating kind, as I winced with pain and repeated, between gasping breaths, "I – don't – know – if – I – can – do – this – again."

Dr. Seng was a highly recommended orthopedic surgeon. After X-rays and an assessment, he calmed me down to a quiet whimper as he diagnosed my fracture as a "general, run-of-the-mill lateral malleolus fracture of the fibula."

He gave me a boot to wear and told me to rest, elevate, and get the swelling down. I would come back in a week to see if the fracture had displaced more and assess from there if I needed surgery to set it. Non-weight-bearing exercises for at least six weeks, he said, which devastated me. Resigned to my fate, I borrowed some crutches and brought my scooter out of storage.

I was in shock. I couldn't believe I was here again. But the survival skills I had gleaned from my last series of injuries came in handy. When I encountered stairs, I immediately sat on my butt and used my arms and elbows to scoot backward up them, dragging my crutches along with me. It was almost easy to balance on

I WAS MADE TO RUN. MY SOUL FEELS IT, MY BODY KNOWS IT, MY HEART LONGS FOR IT. THESE ARE THE THOUGHTS I CHOOSE TO LISTEN TO.

the railing and at the top of the stairs to get my crutches under my arms, then stand up to hobble around my apartment. At least this time I could use crutches.

I immediately mounted a plastic frog—that squeaked when you squeezed him—onto the front of my scooter. The frog was a way to raise my morale, and I laughed when he squeaked as I accidentally hit things around the apartment. But I was far away from happy or optimistic or calm. In every spare moment of the initial weeks after breaking my ankle, I cried at the thought of my recovery and going through the excruciating process once again: recuperating, learning to walk, and gaining back my confidence, which I'd worked so hard to mend. I was overwhelmed with grief and sadness in an intensely raw and helpless way that I never thought I'd experience again.

When I returned to see Dr. Seng a week later, he took more X-rays and thought the safest and best option for me was to have surgery to set the bone with a plate and screws, ensuring a perfect joint alignment of the ankle. Someone with my activity level needed a perfect ankle joint. There was no room for error. I agreed to the surgery, even though it added time to my recovery and inability to bear weight.

Everything was too familiar. The restless night before surgery. The sadness, my quiet grief, the silence of my intense anger, mourning, and inability to control the situation. My mother came to the surgery with me, and it was eerily familiar for the two of us, bringing back memories of a Norwegian hospital bed that seemed too recent to have been forgotten.

It seemed an eternity as I waited for Dr. Seng to come mark my leg up with permanent ink, ensuring no mix-up in the operating room. Every question drew a simple yes or no answer from my mouth, sometimes a shrug. I couldn't form sentences or any more words. Throat thick, eyes welling with unshed tears, I was still overwhelmed to be here again.

The surgery went well enough. No complications or surprises there. But I was surprised by the intensity of my grief. I wasn't ready for this again. I wasn't ready for the familiar feelings of helplessness and dependency. I thought I had learned those skills the first time around. I thought I would be stronger this time, ready to let others help me. Wasn't I stronger? Different now? Didn't I have new skills to get through this setback seamlessly? It was only one bone this time.

I *was* different. The difference after this surgery was that I leaned into grief. I really felt the lows, mourned my loss, and let it run its course. Instead of being depressed for five months, I was ready to tackle my recovery head-on after one week of self-pity and endless tears. I let the wave of emotions come and go. I allowed myself to cry and feel sad, but then committed to be steadfast in my recovery and ignited my belief that I could and would get through it.

This time around, I already had my community, which I leaned into. The day after I broke my ankle I was at Revo again (of course; I had never left). They were my family there. They understood. My good friend Liz Saenz was an angel in disguise . . . or maybe in plain sight. She selflessly took me with her to her own appointments at Revo. Liz was coming back from a hip reconstruction surgery, and she is the definition of perseverance. Every day she picked me up and dropped me off, in the snow, rain, cold, and ice. Every day I crutched out to her car, and we drove to Revo together. We felt like a team. Sometimes we were bright and happy, optimistic, determined. At other times we were somber, crying for no good reason. But we lifted each other up. We were each other's teammates in a time of need. I didn't think it was possible to fall in sync with someone so easily. Liz helped me see the silver lining again, to find the humor in our misery and laugh out loud at the twisted nature of life. She made me stronger and enabled me to keep moving, to get back up, wipe the dirt from my body, and keep moving forward.

In every tough situation there is a lesson. Since my own tough situations came in such close succession and were so similar, it was apparent that I still had something to learn. I wasn't an expert at accepting help. I had always had a hard time relying on other people, and it was tough for me to acknowledge that I had people who loved me for who I was outside of running.

I think that was the most powerful thing I learned through the process of recovering from that second surgery. It taught me, once again, the power of the people you surround yourself with and the importance of immersing yourself in a community that builds you up instead of holding you back or limiting you to just one side of yourself.

I began to feel free and rejuvenated, like a veil was being lifted and I could finally see the obvious. Injuries are painful in that way; they illuminate the areas in your life where improvement or change is necessary. For me, one of those areas was identifying certain people in my life who weren't allowing me to become my best self. This is often hard to realize; I needed a fracture to realize it and recognize that little compromises were slowly adding up to bigger ones, chipping away at my dreams, goals, and aspirations. Compromises which, if I continued to head down the same path, would threaten my core values. The path I was on simply wasn't sustainable.

Change is a constant, and it's endlessly difficult, especially when it involves the dissolution of relationships that were once dear to you. Like breaking a bone, it hurts at first and seems like it will never heal or be the same. But in the end, you grow back stronger. Without these defining moments of enlightenment and challenge, I might have never realized this truth or had the strength to end a relationship and welcome those into my life who encouraged me to be my best self.

Endings are simply punctuations—spaces that separate the old ways from exciting stories and unknown paths. Breaking my ankle helped me navigate this process and allowed me to start fresh, reengage with my strength, and reconnect with those who made me feel most whole. The most challenging moments are a testament to our strength and resilience. They aren't there to knock you down or keep you down. They come to nudge you a little, maybe causing a slip and slide into the mud, but once you get up and clean yourself off, there's always a refreshing perspective to gain, a kind of antifragility.

It's frustrating to feel I'm constantly battling, falling down into the dirt and being forced to get back up and overcome—but I'd really have it no other way. These tough periods in my life have been defining moments, forming my character and showing me what the human spirit, my spirit, is capable of. Without the chance to take those opportunities for a test run, I wouldn't know how strong I am, how capable I am of problem-solving, or how comfortable I can become in the unknown.

Because, after all, we are never done. We are never done overcoming or learning or gaining new perspectives. Would we want to be? Therein lies the beauty, adventure, and wonderful progression of life. We never know what it will bring, but we can have flexibility, mental preparedness, and open perspective, so that when we fall in the dirt, we can get up, clean ourselves off, and choose to become better from it.

That ankle break wasn't easy. The unexpectedness of it really kicked me in the gut. But I tackled it head-on, recommitting myself to physical therapy and recovery and discovering new hobbies. It tested me in a familiar way, but it also led me to see what I was capable of when I shattered in a million broken pieces on the ground. This injury cultivated even more antifragility in my heart, mind, and spirit, which brought pure freedom and joy when I finally was able to run again.

I made a full recovery and started racing during the summer of 2019, a bit later than expected. But I started with a bang, heading back to Cortina yet again to win one of my favorite trail races that June. I called it my comeback race, but it was so much more than that. It was my recovery race.

WHY I RUN

Why do I run? Why do I want to run again? Why did I want to return to something that caused me so much pain?

These are questions I ask myself every day. They are questions I asked myself every day during my recovery, and they are the questions I read in the eyes of my mother, my friends, and my loved ones. Sometimes I didn't understand why I kept going. I didn't always have the answers to these questions. Often, I still can't even put it into words.

Why?

I can't describe the complexity of it, or explain its pure simplicity. It's more a feeling than anything, encapsulated in a repetitive motion, a pattern, as each foot strikes the ground again and again, kicking up dirt, mud or grass, finding their way through the rocks, leaves, and roots. I get lost in that sound. *Pat, pat, pat, pat, pat . . .* complemented by the sound of my breath, whose rhythm changes according to the terrain. My senses are heightened. My mind is cleared, organizing each problem or worry in a perfectly straight path. It's just me, my body, and the earth. So simple, yet multifaceted. I feel like I belong.

Sometimes Mother Nature is quiet, calm, waking up as I pass through her. Other times, she's alive with the buzzing of insects or chirping of birds, the rustling of leaves, or the staleness of summer heat. Each time it is different; the experience is unique, but the feeling is the same. Peace, connectedness, honesty. Even on the most challenging days, I feel this calmness and the gift this movement gives me. I'm brought back to why I run. *I run for this.*

Understanding your why is a concept—a oneness, a state of mind, a state of being. It's like learning something new. At first it doesn't make sense. It's confusing. You have to work at it and study it to comprehend it. But in the end, once you've put in the work, suddenly it's there, beautiful and magnificent, and you can't live without it.

Like anything that is important in our lives, we don't understand the why intellectually at first; we can't categorize or describe it in a discrete way. We just know that it has space and power in our lives, and it feels significant. You may not understand it, but you feel its weight and importance.

This is why I run, why I adventure and go out to push myself day in and day out. I am searching for connection through solitude. I connect with myself, with the spaces I explore, with the human experience and existence itself. Without the extremes I can encounter through running, these playgrounds and experiences of being outside of my comfort zone, I can't feel truly connected or understood—by others or myself. This manner of self-exploration looks different for different people. It can happen through anything that pushes you to be better and really question your purpose here on this earth, causing you to search for the answers within yourself and through your medium.

Around the same time that I made the decision to stop my neuroscience PhD program and pursue my running career instead, I read an article in the *Wall Street Journal* about a Chinese proverb. Actually, my father—the PhD scientist whom I wanted to make proud by getting my PhD—sent me the article in the mail. He had cut it out and sent me a letter. The card read: "I found this article for you to read. Love, Dad." Simple.

The article discussed the tragedy of devoting yourself to only one thing, one pursuit, one passion, one interest. It discussed how life is never that simple. How there needs to be room for balance and other interests and passions to take hold of you and pull you in a different direction—which is often not planned for. It discussed how this makes a person grow and become a full-bodied, rich, enlightened, and intelligent individual.

I called my father to thank him for the article. We talked about life and the different directions it leads us, how it's never straightforward. He told me about his scientific career and how it wasn't textbook or linear at all—there were surprises along the way. He was proud of me for looking inward to see what I really wanted out of life and told me it was smart to pursue my other interests outside science and explore a path that, although not straightforward or guaranteed, was worthwhile for growth, happiness, and discovery.

Throughout my whole life, the challenges I've faced have been pointing me here, nudging me to a looser way of living, where I let my emotions guide me just as my hardheaded stubbornness drives my goals and aspirations. Flexibility, productivity, and being goal-oriented are not mutually exclusive. I used to believe they were, but after enduring my recovery, both mentally and physically, I am now at the point where I realize how important it is to be able to listen to my emotions while I maintain my strong will to perform and achieve.

Listening to this gut feeling, knowing myself, and deep-down acknowledging what I want—or, just as important, what I don't want—can be challenging. And although I've always had gut feelings and the capacity to listen to them, since my accident and subsequent recovery, they've become impossible to ignore. When they show up, I approach them with methodical precision, teasing them apart to understand what they are telling me. Sometimes I don't have a tangible answer or something to grasp or point to. And believe me, that's irritating. I like concrete answers, clear direction. I'm still uncomfortable with the unknown, and taking the time to listen to my emotions sometimes annoys me. But I've learned that these intangible emotions are just as important to engage with as my intellect when making a decision. These gut feelings have taken root in my life. They guide me in all my decisions, professionally and personally, and especially in the mountains.

Listening to these emotional cues has become integral to my athletic health, but also my mental and physical health. If it weren't for my accident, I might not have discovered their importance and learned to engage with them. Recognizing these gut feelings or intuitions when entering the mountains has become especially important for me. There was a great amount of fear in returning to the playground I love. I understood the risk involved in going back to the mountains, but the only way to avoid these risks was to not go to the mountains at all. That was never an option for me.

Instead of avoidance, I became in tune with my intuition, engaging with it, understanding why it's important, and knowing why it's there: to tell me something. There have been many days since my accident when I have planned to take a new route, summit a high peak, or go on a big mountain adventure loop—or sometimes even a run close to home. Most days I feel happy and ready to explore, train, and enjoy. But there are also days when I have a feeling deep within myself, something tapping at my brain, telling me to take a minute that day, to pause.

On these days when it doesn't feel right, when I don't feel right, I decide to change my plans and do something different. This intuition, I believe, is a welcomed result of time and experience spent in the mountains. It's a gift, and an earned consequence of my commitment and dedication to the thing I love. This is respect and the ability to accept the complexity of something I don't understand—to look at the mountains, acknowledge their dominion, regard them, and know they will be there tomorrow. There's no rush. No need to be hasty or lack the patience to take my time and wait until the conditions, both physically and mentally, are (and feel) right. On these days, as difficult as it is to walk away or change plans, I feel the privilege of standing in awe of this world and breathing in its beauty. Some days, it's OK to just look, and maybe, just maybe, if I listen to my intuition the mountains communicate with me and keep me from playing in them for another day.

Over time, I've become more comfortable in the space where I don't know the answers, where I can't plan for the future and don't know what the next few years will be like. Maybe that's scary for some. I think it was scary for me too, at first, and there are days when I'm still uncomfortable in that space. But in many ways, I feel I needed to land here. I was meant to come to this conclusion and this way of living—to let go of what life is "supposed" to look like and embrace what life is, right here and right now.

Running has taught me how to tackle what seems impossible in small, digestible chunks—footsteps, actually. How to problem-solve. How to push through discomfort. How to challenge what I think is possible, to dream, create, and play in the outdoors. Running has taught me love. It's frustrated me beyond belief and yet continues to be both my hardest and easiest activity—sometimes at the same time.

In 2016 I ran in the Buff Epic Trail, the world championships of skyrunning. The 110-kilometer race was a burly one, through the heart of the Pyrenees in northern Spain. This course boasted 26,000 feet of vertical climbing and 26,000 feet of descending. A total elevation change of 52,000 feet over about sixty-eight miles of rocky, rooty, technical single track. It was one of the hardest races I had ever signed up for, and I had prepared well for the challenge. I was going into the race fit and mentally sound. I knew that I could podium if I paced well and executed a good race strategy.

The day before the race, I had the usual jitters, doubts, and anxious energy. My brain was buzzing nonstop, leaping from topic to topic, creating to-do lists for the coming weeks. I couldn't settle down. I had excess energy, with no outlet. I went out for my shakeout run, covering the last five kilometers of the course—I always like to pre-run the finish line, so I can envision the finish and pick out landmarks over the course.

That's a peculiar-looking rock, I think—immediately it's committed to memory. I check my GPS. *Ok, that's 2.3 miles from the finish.* I keep running, feeling fluid and eager to keep going, but I'm nearing the end of my run. I enter a field of wildflowers and spot a bright red ladybug speckled with black spots sunning itself on a yellow flower. Again, I glance at my GPS watch: I'm .75 miles to the finish.

It's part of my routine, committing these small landmarks to memory to provide a mental respite during the final moments of the race, to distract myself from the inevitable pain. I finish my run and stop my watch. I breathe in deeply. Exhale, inhale. Exhale, inhale. Unready to rest, I want to keep going. *This is good, Hillary. Guard the psyche for tomorrow. Guard your energy to the start line.* This was the hardest part for me, the waiting before the start line. Feeling that anxiousness stirring in my stomach, like a flame smoldering, just waiting for more fuel to grow into a raging fire.

"It will be worth it tomorrow during the race," I wrote down in my journal. "You will be happy you rested now, tomorrow. Guard that psyche!" I rested soundly, like I always do before a race, disturbed only by the sound of my alarm at 4 a.m.

I woke up feeling mostly calm, but with the nervous energy persisting. It was my first 110-kilometer race, so that unknown factor scared me. I made myself coffee and breakfast: my typical pre-race oatmeal and fruit. I sat quietly at the table, mentally forming my plan for the race. "Go out comfortable," I said. "Don't push yourself early on; it's a long day and you must pace yourself well. Keep the top five ladies in sight and start making your move at the fifty-kilometer mark."

I walked down to the start of the race, the sun barely peeking over the horizon through the clouds. As rays of orange and yellow streaked across the cloudy sky, I looked up into the silhouettes of the Pyrenees, watching the clouds caress their peaks and valleys. *It will be cold up there today.* I zipped up my jacket to cover my neck and mouth, listening quietly to my footsteps on the ground. As I neared the start line, the noise of the announcer started to boom across the valley, and my walk quickened to a jog as if to match the energy of my surroundings.

As I jogged into the starting corral, the announcer yelled, "Aqui está Hillaryyyy Allennnnn!" I waved to the crowd and greeted my opponents with kisses and hugs. Ten minutes until the start. Cameras flashed, and music blared. I looked to my feet, which were bouncing, and took a few deep breaths . . . inhale . . . exhale . . . inhale . . . exhale . . . I tapped my legs with my hands. *This is the moment you've been waiting for, Hill. You get to run!* I smiled and looked up, cameras flashing in my face, with a minute to go. The countdown song began to play as the crowd grew silent in anticipation.

As the gun went off, we all sprinted forward, eager to encounter the challenge ahead. We made our way through the streets of

Barruera to the start of the single-track trail. There began a conga line of runners, making their way up the first climb of the day. I felt relaxed as I moved. I knew exactly where my competition was, and I was maintaining third position at a very comfortable pace. I was running my own race. *Eat, drink, one step at a time*, I told myself. *Relax and take care of you.*

I executed the first fifty kilometers perfectly. I was still in third place, close to the leading lady, and I was running strong, feeling mentally calm. As I came through the fifty-kilometer checkpoint, feeling happy, my parents were there supporting me, as well as my friend Joan, who was assisting me during the race. He had all my food laid out on a blanket along with Coca-Cola, warm soup, and bubbly water. I refueled, drank, and took some extra food with me. "Thank you," I told them as I left the aid station. "I'll see you at the next one!"

There was a difficult climb between the fifty-kilometer and seventy-kilometer checkpoints. It was long and steep and reached the highest point of the race. The temperature dropped as I climbed, forcing me to put on my jacket and gloves. I topped out at the summit and began to head downhill toward the next checkpoint, but something didn't feel right. It was my stomach.

I drank some water, hoping that would calm it down. *It will pass*, I thought to myself. *It's just the change in temperature and the effort; you're getting into the race now. It's not always going to feel good.* But the feeling persisted and only grew worse as I ticked off the kilometers downhill. I started dry-heaving.

I pulled over to the side of the trail. *What is happening?* I thought. The dry-heaving turned to actual heaving, and everything I had eaten that day was now on the side of the trail. Which also meant I felt a lot better. I drank some water to rinse out my mouth and tried to jog down the trail again. But I wasn't finished. As I vomited again, this time just water came out, with a faint taste of the Skratch gummies I had eaten thirty minutes before.

DETERMINED, I KEPT PUSHING FORWARD.

Shit, I thought to myself. *You've got to keep moving; try to make your way to the aid station and refuel there. You'll feel better, don't worry.* I wasn't sure if I had eaten too much or eaten something that was "off" or if it just wasn't my day, but I was in bad shape as I continued to run down the trail.

It was then that I realized the next aid station wasn't at the end of this descent. I still had to climb over the next pass and descend it to reach aid, to reach my parents and Joan. I had to make it there to replenish the calories I had just lost. *You just have to get to them, Hill.*

Determined, I kept pushing forward, relentlessly moving my feet up and over the next pass and down to the next aid. But my body felt hollow, empty. I couldn't push. When I arrived, I was exhausted and in severe caloric deprivation. I needed energy, and I needed it fast. I didn't know how I was going to keep moving or if I should even keep going. How was I going to finish the race? I still had forty kilometers to cover. How could I do that if I couldn't eat any food? I felt like giving up. I looked to Joan and my parents. My mother's face wore a worried expression as she handed me water. She said nothing, but I knew what she was thinking. The same as me. Wondering if I should I keep going. *Do I give up now?* At this point, I had slipped into the fifteenth position, and all I wanted was to pull out of the race.

But then, between gulps of water, bites of saltine crackers, and sips of ginger ale, a thought entered my fuzzy mind: *Do I want to quit because I'm not winning, or do I want to quit because I don't feel good?*

As I sat in the aid station tent, wallowing in self-pity and doubt, I started to cry—for my upset stomach, for how shitty I felt, and for the race, which I felt was slipping away. All of my hard work and preparation, I felt, was for nothing.

I looked to my parents, who had flown all this way to watch me race and were driving the winding roads of the Pyrenees all day and night to crew for me and bring me food. I looked to Joan, also investing his time in me, helping me run this race.

As I gazed into the faces of my people, I knew I couldn't quit. I had to find a way to keep moving forward. To keep going, set aside my pride, and finish this thing.

Summoning the energy and courage to stand up, I put on my running pack—now stuffed with saltines and ginger ale—and walked out the door.

The next few hours weren't pretty. In fact, they got pretty ugly. I couldn't eat much. A few hundred yards out of the aid station, I threw up everything again. Over the next few hours, if I drank too much ginger ale, I threw up. If I pushed too hard up the climbs, I buckled over dry-heaving on the side of the trail. The best pace I could muster was a solid power-hiking grind up the steep climbs and a gentle trot on the downhills to the valley floor below.

I could see the aid stations from miles away and hear my mother's cheer echoing through the corridors of the towering Pyrenees. Each aid station was fifteen to twenty kilometers from the last, taking anywhere between three and four hours to reach.

Eventually, I reached each one. Every time I stepped into an aid station to meet with my team, I'd sit down and let the tears rush over me. Thoughts of quitting clouded my mind. I was drained, and every ounce of me wanted to quit.

This wasn't worth it. It's too hard! I can't do it. These thoughts played on repeat as I sucked on ginger candies and swallowed sips of Coca-Cola. Joan rubbed my back and said, "Estas bien, Hillary, si se puede!" He handed back my running pack, stuffed with more ginger ale and saltine crackers, passed me my trekking poles, and escorted me to the door. I didn't know where the determination was coming from. But I buckled my pack, took my trekking poles in my hands, and, inexplicably, headed out to the flagged trail ahead. I couldn't quit. I just couldn't give up.

The rest of the course was as brutal as the first part: unrelenting climbs and steep, technical descents. My pace remained the same, along with my lack of fueling. The hours accumulated along with the fatigue in my legs. As I made my way to the base of the final climb, the sun was beginning to set. I pulled out my headlamp, securing it to my head, and put my head down as I inched my way up the climb. I hadn't seen many people all day, but as the sun faded away behind the mountains, headlamps began illuminating the paths of my competitors above me on the trail.

I kept my pace, head down, light shining, focusing on just the fifteen feet ahead of me and before I knew it, there were two running feet in front of me. "Disculpe," or sorry, I said as I passed them, not even looking up to see if it was a man or a woman.

I grinded in this rhythm for more than an hour up the final climb. Once I reached the top, I finally raised my head, looking to the clear, starry night above. There was a security checkpoint here, and the volunteer recorded my number as I began the long descent down to Barruera. I wasn't focused on the pain anymore. I still couldn't eat, and the emptiness of my stomach now felt like a permanent cavity in my body, but I kept running. I kept going. Focusing on the relief of the finish line that would eventually come.

I passed through a final aid station. Trying to take a sip of Coke, I dry-heaved again. My face crumpled into a grimace. I wanted to cry, but there was no water in my body to produce the tears. There were only five kilometers left. I couldn't believe my legs were still moving. I could hardly find the energy to open my eyes, yet every time I looked down, my legs were moving forward, in a running motion. *How am I doing this? I just want it to be over.* My headlamp illuminated the path before me as I listened to the pitter-patter of my feet, each step getting me closer to the finish line.

As the cheering and noise of the announcer grew nearer, I finally saw it. The finishing tent, with its red and black flags. I sighed with relief, a full-body sigh that instantly made me sob. I was going to finish. As I continued to run, I recognized my mother's cheers in the crowd, then my father's. I couldn't see their faces. I hadn't seen anything except the path of my headlamp for hours. Nothing else existed. As I crossed the finish line I collapsed on the ground, the complete and utter exhaustion I had been feeling all day finally engulfing me whole. But in that moment, I knew I had done the right thing. I had fought until the very end, and the feeling of satisfaction as I crossed the line made it one of the best moments of my life. All the suffering was worth that moment.

In the end, it was seventeen hours I miserably pressed through, struggling both mentally and physically as I fought my way from aid station to aid station. I even clawed my way back to fifth place. That day, I found out what I was capable of. I learned what I could endure, what I could come back from. I learned to swallow my pride and finish something I started. There's no other way I could have learned those valuable lessons that day. If my race had gone perfectly, or if I had given up when things went south, I would have never known how much I could endure or overcome to get to that finish line.

So why? Why do I need to run and why do I want to run again? Through one of the most difficult experiences of my life, I was finally able to understand these reasons and why I had to keep coming back.

Running simply makes me better. It makes me a whole person, able to engage with all the parts of me. It's not just about being a runner, the act of running, being an athlete, training, and going from one race to the next. That's too simple, too narrow, and leaves no room for growth. Running has become a place where I can explore every part of me. It's one of the few places where I can struggle, suffer, cry, hit rock bottom, and still become better. It's one of the few places where I can learn about the most important relationship in my life—my relationship with myself. This relationship is perpetually evolving and in constant need of love and attention, but through running, movement, and challenge, I've discovered the best way to take care of me. The best way to allow myself the space to grow, change, and love, and to be confused, uncomfortable, and raw—with no timeline or hidden agenda. In doing so, I'm able to perform at my best, to be honest and authentic with everyone I come in contact with.

Of course, I'm not perfect and life is never clear-cut, but thanks to the skills I cultivate through running, I can tackle life's obstacles. Running gives me the confidence of knowing I can handle any tough situation.

I think honestly knowing oneself and exploring the depths of our human experience is the most difficult task, yet remains the most rewarding one. Running is how I deal with the unexpected, celebrate the new, embrace the exciting; it's how I grieve, contemplate, experiment, confront, rediscover, relax, and rise above. It's the why behind everything I do, and without it I wouldn't be the same me I'm constantly discovering.

12 GOING BACK TO TROMSØ

When I thought about going back to Tromsø, Norway—back to that ridgeline—fear took over. I always thought that someday I'd be ready, and I would just know it was time to go back. I thought the progression of mental and physical recovery would be routine, and I'd be able to make the journey and confront my fear. That's not the case at all. Recovery is anything but straightforward, but the twists and turns add to its meaning and to the beauty and delightful surprises you find along the way.

At the beginning of 2019, I felt "ready" to go back to Tromsø. I felt strong again, mentally and physically. I felt ready to tackle not only a running season, but the challenges of my trauma. I had begun to entertain the idea of going back to Tromsø, not just to see the ridge, but to do the race. I started planning and talking to race directors. But then I broke my ankle—and with it my confidence.

After I broke my ankle, I decided my overarching theme for 2019 would be *do things that scare me*. This was definitely true for my first race back after breaking my ankle, the Cortina Trail. I lacked confidence in my speed, I hadn't been running as much as I would have liked leading into an ultrarace, and I was afraid of the technical terrain in the Dolomites.

Could my ankle handle it? Would I twist it again, or hurt myself some other way? Could my body hold up? I got on that start line anyway, and I ran with heart, joy, and appreciation. When I came across that finishing tape in first place at Cortina, feeling strong, capable, and happy, I knew I was returning to Tromsø. Not to try to win the race, or to keep to some sort of timeline in my recovery, but because it scared me; it challenged me, and I didn't feel ready to go back. I sent a message to my coach that night telling him I wanted to go back. He said it felt right and supported my decision.

As I made plans to go to Tromsø, contacting the race directors and my sponsors, telling my friends and family, I certainly had my doubts. Was this the right thing to do? Was I ready? Physically and emotionally? I didn't know how I was going to feel up on that ridge. Would I be able to do it? Would I be able to complete the race? Would it happen again?

I decided to ask my friend Manu to join me during the race. I didn't want to do the race at a race pace, but I wanted to complete it as a celebration of coming full circle. Manu was the first person on the scene when I fell, scrambling down to me on the ridgeline to make sure I was OK. He helped with the rescue operation and visited me in the hospital in the days following. We kept in touch and regularly touched base throughout my recovery. Going back to this race and doing it with Manu would provide some closure for us both.

But in the days and weeks leading up to the race, my mind wavered. Although I was committed to going back, waves of fear crashed over me, causing doubt. I wondered if this was the fear I needed to push through or the fear I needed to listen to, the kind of fear that was telling me to stay away for good reason. I wondered if it was my gut, that inner voice I had learned to listen to, telling me to steer clear to keep myself out of danger. Or was it something else? Was it fear of past trauma causing a reactionary resistance to revisiting a place that nearly killed me? It was hard to tell the difference, honestly. The feelings felt so similar.

These questions plagued my mind for several days. But after intentional thought and consideration, I knew it was the latter. My body and mind were trying to protect me. It was different from intuition, which was a calm voice, nudging me to pay attention because something didn't feel right. This other fear came from a panicked and reactive place. It was a protective impulse. I knew I had to go back, unless I wanted to hold on to that tension. I didn't.

The first step in my return to Tromsø during the summer of 2019 was returning to the skyrunning circuit. It was the series that had put me on the map, ignited my love for running, and sparked my creative way of exploring the world as I raced. While I had returned to racing, I hadn't returned to the skyrunning circuit. Although I had planned to do the 2019 season, with the ankle break in January I canceled all my race season plans so I could focus on healing. After my first race back at Cortina Trail in June, that gut feeling was pulling me back into it all. So, in addition to going back to Tromsø, I also signed up for my first skyrunning race, the Royal Ultra SkyMarathon Gran Paradiso fifty-five-kilometer race in Gran Paradiso National Park, Italy.

I decided this would be a training run. My goal would be to go out there and celebrate being able to move. This would relieve some of the pressure I often put on myself. These courses are pretty technical and rugged, and I knew race day would be an exciting and overwhelming experience. I didn't know just how overwhelming it would be.

The Italian winter had been long, and there was still snow on the course. A week before the race, the race organization announced that it was mandatory for runners to bring running traction for certain sections of the race where there was still snow. I'd run plenty of times in microspikes, but this made my heart jump. It would be my first time running on snow since breaking my ankle. The idea terrified me.

The day before the race, I rented a car to drive to the national park. I was staying in Annecy, France, for the summer, and Gran Paradiso was a short drive through the Mont Blanc tunnel to the Italian side of the Alps. As I waited in the line of cars to cross through the Mont Blanc tunnel I had a breakdown. Without warning, I began to cry, and then sob. My body felt panicked, and my mind was racing, searching for a reason to turn back. *The traffic! It's a training run; I should just run somewhere else by myself to take the pressure off. The snow! I don't want to hurt my ankle again.* I turned around in the line of cars and pulled over on the side of the road, now uncontrollably sobbing.

Gripping the steering wheel, I couldn't decide what to do. My hazard lights flashed as I idled on the side of the road. Finally, I turned off the car and, as I removed my hands from the steering wheel to wipe my eyes, decided to call my coach. I texted him first—it was 3 a.m. in Boulder—but within a minute he texted back. I had caught him as he was going to pee in the middle of the night. I called and Adam listened to me sob as I told him I didn't know what to do.

"Hill, I know you're scared," he said calmly. "I know the snow scares you and going back to this series scares you, but this is something you need to do. You need to take this step before returning to Tromsø. Take a deep breath, turn the car around, and get yourself to Italy. You can do this. I believe in you. This isn't practical fear. This is a normal fear to have. Everything will be OK. You need to believe in yourself. I do! Now get yourself to Italy and call me when you finish this race. You can do it, Goat."

I nodded, sniffling. "I can do this."

I turned the hazard lights off and restarted my car. I turned around and headed through the tunnel into Italy.

I arrived an hour before the race debrief. Just enough time to catch a shakeout run with my roommate Antonia, whom I had just met. She had no idea who I was or what coming back to a sky-running event meant to me. We exchanged small talk during our thirty-minute jog.

"I've been to three Olympic games in cross-country skiing," she said. "I just found running two years ago."

I was impressed and couldn't wait to tell my coach, who had a background in cross-country skiing. My mind was finally distracted from the pressure of "my return." After our jog, I entered the room where the race debriefing was being held, scanning the room and taking note of familiar faces. *There's Ragna—she won the Skyrunner World Series the year of my accident. She is still racing strong. There's Pere too; he looks as strong as ever.* I hadn't seen these faces in two years.

"Wow, Hillary, here you are! The last time I saw you was on your scooter," Ragna said in her thick Catalan accent. "I knew you would be back." She squeezed my hand and smiled. "You are very brave to come back to the series. I wish you a very good race tomorrow."

All I could do was nod and smile. "Thank you," I managed to squeeze out. No words could encapsulate my happiness, and simultaneous apprehension, over coming to this race. I stood in reluctance, accepting all the conflicting emotions as they washed over me. I took a deep breath and exhaled, releasing the tension. Then my eyes caught the supportive gaze of Lauri van Houten and Marino Giacometti, a married couple and founders of the Skyrunner World Series. They had helped me enter the world circuit and build my career as a runner. They were also there when the accident happened and, although they had followed along in my recovery, we hadn't seen each other in two years.

"Bella! Bella! Ciao, Hillary!" Marino cried as he grabbed my face between his hands and kissed my cheeks. He embraced me in a warm hug. "I'm so happy to see you! I'm so glad you are here with us." Tears brimmed in his eyes as he passed me over to his wife.

"Hillary, I'm so thrilled to see you," Lauri said as she hugged me. "What a brave woman you are." We chatted for the remainder of the evening, catching up on life. As I returned to my room later that night, I knew I had come for the right reasons. Tomorrow's race was more than just a "return" to the series, or a certain finish time or place. It was something beyond words. It was another chapter in my healing process.

Antonia and I woke up at 4 a.m. the day of the race. We already had all our gear ready: running packs with full water bottles, our race fuel, and all the mandatory equipment for the race. My microspikes were accessible in the upper part of my pack. I triple-checked I had everything and started putting on the race kit lying neatly next to my pack. Ten minutes later, Antonia and I headed down to breakfast, ordering extra double espressos. We were both feeling relaxed and excited for the race.

"How did you sleep?" I asked Antonia as I sipped my coffee between bites of oatmeal.

"Very well," she said. "I think this will be a good day." We both looked outside to the clear, starry predawn sky above. Not a cloud in sight.

After breakfast we made our way to the bus stop one hundred meters down the street from our hotel, where we waited silently in the dark as other runners stumbled up to join us. Once on the bus, we began the twisting ride up to the start of the race, entering Gran Paradiso National Park. The race started at 2,500 meters. For me this was nothing, but some of the racers commented on the "altitude." As I exited the bus and began to shake out my legs I felt a wave of excitement pulse through my body. Ultramarathons are unpredictable. During a race I can experience everything—from good feelings to really bad lows, plagued by tears and self-doubt. I actually enjoyed not knowing how it would turn out before starting the race.

I wasn't sure what my day was going to be like, but as the race

> RUNNING AT MY OWN PACE, I TOLD MYSELF OVER AND OVER AGAIN, "THIS IS WHAT STRENGTH LOOKS LIKE."

director started to count down from ten—nine, eight, seven—that electric excitement concentrated in my legs. Three, two, one. *Bang!* I started running up the first climb, feeling calm and relaxed. Running at my own pace, I told myself over and over again, "This is what strength looks like." When another woman passed me or thoughts about the impending snow and ice popped into my head I kept repeating, "This is what strength looks like. You've started, you're here. Keep moving forward." *But the snow*, I thought. *How will it be?* "Fear. This is what strength looks like. You're confront-ing fear." *What if I don't place well?* "Courage. This is what strength looks like. You're doing this for you, not anyone else."

As we climbed, the path transformed from runnable single track to rocky terrain and big boulder fields. I transitioned from a run to a hike as I hopped and climbed over boulders the size of small cars. It comforted me, reminding me of home. I focused on that warm memory as the trail turned completely snow-covered and we reached the pass. A mountain guide hired for race security was there instructing everyone, "Put on your crampons. They are required until the next checkpoint."

The snow, soft and wet, was already melting with the rising sun. *This is good, Hillary, you don't have to worry about ice.* My foot punched through the snow, hitting a rock in the covered boulder field below. I took a deep breath, but I still couldn't relax. Like a drum pounding louder and louder, my anxiety grew. I wanted off this snow, but it kept stretching farther and farther out beneath my feet.

Other racers, more comfortable with the risk of falling, slid and barreled past me. This also made me nervous, as I didn't want them to crash into me. My heart pounded loud in my chest. I didn't feel comfortable. I could feel my face grow flushed. As I approached a roped section with more mountain guides securing the line below, I knew I was visibly panicked and upset. *What's wrong with me? Why are you crying?* I whimpered as I made my way slowly down the fixed line. I could see the clear trail below. I finally exhaled and managed to eke out a smile for the security volunteers. They, as well as a few other runners, knew who I was.

"Hillary, you are very brave."

"Keep going."

With every word of encouragement, I smiled, and my sobbing slowly diminished as I kept going. But I was still in a low spot. Judging myself and my ability. Cursing my awkward feet and hesitation. *I was once so strong! What happened to me?* I wanted to be alone. Not crowded by all these people. *Should I just quit? Should I just do the shorter course?* I wondered, knowing the turning point for the shorter course was soon approaching. I looked at my watch: 2:05 was my moving time. *Holy shit, I've still got a long way to go. You need to change your mindset if you want to get through this.*

I had topped out on the second pass when I began to cry again as I slipped and awkwardly navigated the second downhill. As I was cry-running my way slowly down over the snow and rocks, an Italian runner came up behind me. He heard my tears and gently tapped my shoulder as he passed me.

"Forza!" he said, along with something else I didn't understand in Italian. He stopped and gently took my face, looking me straight in the eyes. "You can do this! You are strong! Brave!" I nodded. As he turned to start running, I wiped the tears from my face and followed in his footsteps.

Forza, Hillary, you can do this.

I decided on a new race strategy. Do what I could on the downhills, staying safe and as relaxed as I could, then push on the uphills. *Uphills are your thing, Hillary.*

This took the pressure off. I stopped at the aid stations. I tried to speak Italian with the volunteers. I ate cake and Italian cookies, and drank bubbly water and tea. My eyes marveled at the views of spectacular meadows, mountain passes, and clear mountain lakes and rivers. *When will you ever have a chance to run in a place like this? Enjoy it. Remember the details.*

I ran by a family of mountain ibex, scampering up the vertical rock with ease. I waved hello, wishing their agility into my own feet. I breathed in the fresh scent of minerals and mountain air. Hours passed by like the clear mountain streams—fluid, uninterrupted, easy. I felt small as I gazed up at those towering mountains, their jagged granite peaks, like animal teeth, piercing the sky. I wasn't threatened by their hostility. Instead I felt safe, protected by the green valley floor below, the soft belly of Mother Nature. I felt like I was healing.

As I topped out on the final climb and made my way down the final descent, I started laughing. The descent was difficult. I kept twisting my ankles, unable to see where to place my foot in the overgrown, rocky trail. I just wanted to be done. My watch beeped as it totaled another kilometer. I held up my wrist to see the total: fifty-five kilometers. "Where's the finish line then?" The race was supposed to be done at fifty-five kilometers. I burst into laughter again at the familiar feeling of frustration. I laughed at my anger about the extra kilometers. I laughed because this was inevitable in an ultra, that longing for the finish line. But more than anything, I laughed because I was happy to be experiencing this exhaustion again. I had earned the fatigue, the frustration, the readiness to be done. I felt incredibly full of exhaustion, pride, and accomplishment.

I ran with those feelings for those extra five kilometers. As I rounded the final corner and saw the finishing tent, I began to cry again. But those tears came from the fullness of the journey I had just made. I had overcome my own fear and doubt. I had ignored expectation and let go of pride. My heart needed this, and so did my soul. Because once again I learned what I was capable of. I crossed the finish line and embraced Lauri and Marino, who wiped the tears from my face. Each kissed me on the cheek. We didn't need to say anything . . . our silent emotional exchange said it all.

I don't consider myself an especially brave person. I'm definitely not a daredevil or adrenaline junkie. I like plans and routines. I like to assess the risks of the situations in front of me. I have two strict rules in life: 1) don't huck anything (this mainly applies to running, cycling, and skiing), and it generally keeps me safe; and 2) no talking about food until you're five kilometers from the finish line (for running) or thirty minutes from the finish (for cycling or skiing). I abide by these rules. I practice them daily. We have an understanding, these rules and I. But as I've been tackling my recovery and living my life as a survivor, trying to rediscover my identity and place in this world, both competitively and personally, I keep hearing the word "brave."

This confuses me a bit, or catches me by surprise. I don't view myself this way. Instead, I see it more as me stubbornly finding a way to live and go after what I want, after what makes me feel alive, happy, and full of life experiences. If all of that makes me brave, then I guess I'll have to start seeing myself in that light too.

It gives me strength to say that I'm brave. Especially as I faced thoughts of returning to that ridge in Norway. To that spot where I nearly died.

What does it look like? What will it feel like? Will I be able to stand there, to stand in the emotions? Will I recognize it? Will I feel anything at all? What if it happens again?

All these questions gave me pause. I tried to ignore the most pressing question, but my brain kept asking it. *What if it happens again, Hillary? What if you're up on that ridge and you fall again?* I wanted to stop my mind from going there, focusing instead on the emotional release I would experience by confronting my fear.

Brave. *You're brave, Hillary. It's good you're going back. It will be a release, a good thing for your mind, your soul, your body.* Then, suddenly it returned—the unwelcome thought—what if it happens again?

I couldn't ignore it. And did I want to? Did I want to ignore the honesty I felt? Did I want to pretend I wasn't afraid of falling off that ridge again? I couldn't pretend that fear wasn't there. That was part of the reason I was going back to that spot, to challenge this fear and form new memories, a new experience—both alone and, during the race, with the people who were there with me the last time. I was going to confront my fears, look them straight in the face, and shape a different outcome.

I didn't know what I would experience when I encountered them, yet I was eager to find out. To be brave. To say *yes* to the fear. But this bravery, this courageous confrontation, didn't stop the nightmares. Nor did it stop the spiraling of my thoughts or the wondering if I should go back. I didn't think going back to that spot would really transform me, nor did I think it was necessary to return to that ridge in order to move on with my life. I felt whole without that. I felt content in my journey, knowing what I had learned and continued to learn. I was not the same person I was two years ago, so I was going back to see it from a new perspective, a different perspective. I was going back as the new me.

When I arrived in Tromsø, it was an eerie feeling. I recognized the airport, the city, the hotel, the sun that never sets when you're this far north in the Artic. The landscape was familiar, a high alpine aesthetic at sea level, with fjords snaking in and out of the mountains.

I met Manu to go up on Hamperokken Ridge. I hadn't seen him in two years. We'd kept in contact throughout my recovery, supporting each other from afar, but the last time I saw him was in the hospital after I fell from that cliff.

I wanted to go back there together and see where I fell. Manu picked me up at the hotel and we caught up on life as we made our way to the ridge. Later, Manu told me that it was surreal to see me standing in front of him that day, because the last time he'd seen me I was in a wheelchair.

As we pulled up to the parking lot for the mountain, I recognized the trail and the spot where I fell.

"There was an aid station there," I said as we tied our shoes, "and we ran this way up the mountain." Manu nodded. As we started running toward the single track in the forest, I turned to him. "Can you tell me about the accident, about what happened and about what you did? I want to know everything."

Manu was polite, letting me lead the conversation, considerate of my feelings and aware that I might not want to talk about what happened. We hadn't had the chance, in two years, to go over what he experienced, what we experienced together.

As we made our way up the trail, rising onto the ridgeline, Manu told me that he didn't see what happened, what caused me to trip or fall; he just saw me falling. He was about ten meters behind me, and what he remembers is the sound of my body hitting the rocks over and over again.

"The sound still haunts me today," he said. After I fell, Manu didn't see me stop; he just kept hearing the crashes.

"I didn't think," he said. "I just started climbing down the cliff to find you."

When he did, he was met with a horrible sight. Manu was sure I was dead. So sure that he didn't even check for a heartbeat or to see if I was breathing. My body was contorted. My back was arched and clearly broken. My ribs and ribcage were bent in ways a human body shouldn't be bent. And my shoes. One of them was completely missing—flown off my foot and somewhere down the mountainside. The other shoe was nearby, the bottom completely shredded, barely looking like a shoe anymore. There were gaping wounds, and so much blood everywhere.

My body lay on the snow, but I was near another cliff edge. One slight movement and I would fall again. Manu realized he needed to move me so that wouldn't happen. When he got close, he realized I was still breathing. That's when his focus and wilderness training kicked in. He suspected my back was broken, so he stabilized my neck and put his legs under my body as he scooted me away from the ledge and seated us in the snow. My head was bleeding a lot, and he only had his running jacket and the emergency blanket he had found in my running pack. He used his jacket to cover my head wound and draped my body in the emergency blanket. There was a huge gash on my leg. The scars have slightly faded over the years, but they are still quite prevalent, reminding me of the wound's severity.

I asked Manu about the scars. He grimaced and pointed to my right quad muscle. "That one, that one was deep. Your leg was totally open, and I could have put my hand sideways inside your leg."

Manu was applying pressure with his own forehead to the gash in my head, holding me with one arm, and using his other hand to try to hold shut the gash in my leg. The other cuts in my legs, although big and gaping, weren't bleeding that much.

Somewhere between Manu moving me from the edge, covering my head, and holding together my leg, I started to wake up. His face was close to mine, holding pressure on the cut on my forehead with his head as he held my leg shut with his hand. When I saw him in the hospital later, still in a daze of drugs and pain, that was the first thing I said to him: "I remember your face close to mine."

Manu told me how hard I was fighting. How I was in so much pain but trying my best to do what he told me. I kept raising my arms because they hurt. I was screaming and mumbling, "Help me! It hurts!" Manu grabbed my hand and told me to try not to move them. He could see the concentration in my face as I stayed still, until the next wave of pain came through. Manu kept holding my hand, even though it made him stick to his stomach. "It was like holding a loose bag of bones," Manu told me. My arms and hands weren't hands or arms, just skin with broken bones floating around inside.

Manu told me that right then, on the side of the mountain, he saw who I really was. He saw how strong I was, how determined I was to survive and fight. The strongest person he had ever met—something he had also shared in a note he left me in the hospital, one I still keep on a bulletin board above my bed and read every night before I go to sleep.

We were complete strangers on that ridge, and we really don't even know each other that well now, yet, at the same time, we knew each other deeply. I trusted Manu like I've trusted no one in my life before. I trusted him with my life—in that terrible moment on the side of the ridge and now, as we run onto Hamperokken Ridge, two years after the accident, to see the place where I fell and nearly lost my life.

As we rose higher, the steep grass shoulder of the mountain started to fragment into granite boulders until we were on the ridge itself, sharp and jagged with impressive rock. Manu traced the ridge and pointed out to me the point at which I fell. I saw the ridge, a series of three jagged summits, for the first time in two years.

He pointed to the first jagged summit and said, "That's where you fell, right there from the top, and you see that snowfield below? That's where I found you and braced you in the snow."

I stood in awe. It was so far that I had fallen. I looked at Manu and he could read my expression. "Yes, you fell that far! Fifty meters is a long way!" We continued on the ridge at a deliberate pace, my eyes meticulously on Manu's path, nearing the spot where I fell.

I asked him about the helicopters and how long it took. "Maybe thirty minutes," he said. The longest thirty minutes of his life. Once those doctors came, he felt like he could finally relax, that it was no longer his job to keep me safe; he had help now. He could breathe again. But it took a while for the doctors to get things in order. The helicopter had no place to land, so the doctors talked about moving me up to the ridge—an impossible task.

The helicopter spent what seemed like an eternity hovering up on the ridge, moving loose rocks from the top, which came crashing down around us. Finally, they decided to lower a rope (which was barely long enough) to attach to a cot and hoist me up into the helicopter. After they took me away, Manu was shaken and in shock. He ran down with Kilian back to the aid station, covered in blood . . . my blood. It took him a long time to recover his confidence. Technical and mountain terrain was his favorite type of terrain, but after my accident it took him nearly two years to regain his own strength, mentally, on this terrain.

Manu had done the Hamperokken skyrace the year after my accident, to rid himself of his own demons and close his own loop. That's what I was attempting to do as we stood on the ledge where I fell. Looking down at the vertical terrain, I didn't cry. I just observed. I looked around for answers, an explanation of what caused me to fall. I saw nothing, felt nothing. No release. I found no answers. All I could do was gaze upon the spot, the mountainside, and then look to Manu in silent astonishment and disbelief that he was able to climb down to me to help me, disbelief that I am alive now and on this ridge again. We continued on the ridge in silence. As we reached the summit of Hamperokken Ridge, I shed tears of simultaneous joy, fear, and release.

I sat in silence for most of that evening, unable to process or even pinpoint exactly what I was feeling. I felt numb, an odd emptiness. I didn't feel free. Being on the ridgeline again didn't bring fear, but an uneasiness, a gut feeling of discomfort and restlessness. I didn't want to go back there. Not ever again. Not during the race. Not ever. I wanted to leave Norway right away.

I sat with these emotions, trying to explore them. I slept on them, to see how I felt the next day. When I woke up the following morning and tried to write about the experience, the tears came. They flowed uncontrollably as I thought about Manu's words, the ridge, how bad the accident really was, and how amazing it was that I was there now, experiencing Norway all over again.

I met up with Manu again later that day to run through the forest to a small peak near his cabin in the woods. We spent the afternoon together, talking, laughing, getting to know each other, and playing with his two dogs. I didn't realize it until later that night, but I was forming new memories. This might sound trivial, but I believe that when I first arrived, the stress of returning to Hamperokken Ridge during the skyrace was inseparable from my memories of two years ago, my past experience in Tromsø. I hadn't yet been able to enjoy this place and the people. I hadn't been able to see the beauty of the landscape. My memories were riddled with fear and a vague, piercing pain. Spending time with Manu and my friends, exploring Norway as a wonderful playground filled with adventure and wild freedom, was allowing me to disassociate from my previous experience there.

Over the course of a couple of days—after seeing the ridge and being there for the first time, feeling so uncomfortable and out of place, not wanting to go back, wanting to leave Norway, feeling anxious, lacking confidence—my emotions transformed. What started as fear and hesitation, anger and doubt—thoughts that this mountain had forever taken my strength and love of mountain running—transformed into progress.

Forming new memories with my friends and family surrounding me, laughing big belly laughs as we climbed up new mountains and visited new fjords, nooks, and crannies, injected happiness into a place that had been the source of my nightmares for two years. To receive the love and support of those closest to me, and from a community of runners I hardly knew, yet who somehow felt like a part of me, was a liberating experience. It reminded me why I came back and why I love to run. It reminded me of the importance of exploration and what pushing limits really means—both physically and emotionally.

I remembered why I came back to this place, and by the time Saturday morning came along, I felt ready and happy to be on that start line. As the clock counted down the final minutes and seconds to the race and Manu and I took off together toward

Hamperokken Ridge, I thought to myself, *This is my day. I'm going to finish this race. I know it won't be easy, but I'm ready to do this.*

In the end, we did the whole race. There were tears, belly laughs, stories, silence, enjoyment, suffering, smiles, and doubts, but in the end, we supported one another—and we made a damn good team. I never thought I'd smile that much on Hamperokken Ridge or receive such positive support from volunteers and other racers, who were in awe of my return. The race certainly wasn't straightforward, and at times I felt like it would never end, this cloud, hanging over me for the past two years. But Manu and I worked together to build each other up in the lows and celebrate in the highs—and managed not to kill each other by the end. We had a lot of fun and shared some pretty hilarious moments we'll keep reliving for years to come. Most importantly, we managed to follow both our rules for the run that day:

Rule #1: Don't talk about food until we are five kilometers from the finish (both Manu and I follow this rule religiously in training and races . . . who knew?!).

Rule #2: No more talking about the accident. We are both so much more than one bad day in the mountains.

Crossing that finish line and hugging my mother and Manu was one of the sweetest moments of my life. I had closed the loop. I had conquered my fears and confronted them head-on. As I felt the warm rush of relief and satisfaction course through my body, I smiled and laughed. Looking around at the faces of the runners, volunteers, and supporters, I thought to myself, *Thank you. Thank you for fighting for yourself, for not giving up, for reminding yourself and others what you can do, what we can do, when we challenge what we think is possible.*

EPILOGUE

At the beginning of the year, I felt broken. By now, you know the story: a nearly fatal accident that threatened my running career, building myself back up, recovering, refusing to give up on my dream, learning about myself . . . only to break my ankle just eighteen months later and start all over again.

I've experienced too many moments of raw emotion to summarize the complete brokenness of my body and spirit or the journey I've undertaken. I've tried to do that as best as I can in the pages of this book, through stories and by inviting you into my mind and heart to understand my personal process of rebuilding. My hope is to challenge you to do the same in your own life.

The unexpected has certainly changed my life, transformed me and opened me up in ways I never thought possible. I've had to look fear in the face several times and choose to keep moving forward, despite not knowing what my future would look like. After breaking my ankle in the midst of my recovery, I hit a new low. I had overcome all the odds to return to run at an elite level, but this injury impacted my confidence and left me questioning everything, wondering if I could do it again.

Despite all the doubts, the pain, and the changes in plans, I found a way through. I found my stride again. I found what makes me happy, my reason to keep trying and keep pursuing my dreams, even if I might fail.

I had a lofty goal for my post-recovery: I wanted to do the longest race I had ever done in my entire career. It was a crazy thing. After my accident and subsequent recovery, I discovered another gear. I put in the longest training runs and weeks I had ever done in my ultrarunning career, something that was spectacular to see, and I was excited to try something I had never done before: a 145-kilometer (91-mile) race through the Alps in Italy and France. This race, called TDS (Tour du Duc de Savoie) boasts 9,100 meters of climbing (nearly 30,000 feet) through technical, remote mountains. It's one of the hardest and most competitive races in the world.

The adventure of the course drew me in. I was excited by it. I felt like I had been preparing well for it, but when I broke my ankle, my entire plan was thrown. I had just started my training block for the season, but with another surgery, I wouldn't able to bear any weight for six weeks. It wasn't until that April 2019 that I was able to start hiking, and not until the middle of April that I was able to start running. I wasn't sure I'd be ready by that August to do TDS—a race that not only requires peak fitness, but strong ankles, due to the technical terrain and unrelenting distance. I was full of doubt. But for some reason I didn't take TDS off my schedule. I kept my name on that starting list, in hopes that I would be ready. Maybe subconsciously I had faith in myself, and even though I would encounter doubt every day, I believed I would be ready.

That summer I moved to France for two months to train on the racecourse. To see its burliness for myself. Running on those trails scared me more than anything. My ankle hurt, thanks to all the vertical ups and downs. And the miles crawled by, thanks to the technical trails. I put in some of my hardest training days ever, both mentally and physically. And still, I didn't feel ready. This race was thirty-one miles longer than any race I had ever done. I had competed in two one-hundred-kilometer races before, but that was in 2016, before my accident. Since then, I hadn't had the confidence or the strength to do a longer race.

So, preparing for TDS was far more than physical for me. I kept a journal and wrote down my fears and doubts about the race, trying to mentally prepare myself and wrap my head around this new challenge.

Just about every other day I would text my coach: "ADAM, CAN I DO THIS?? It's nearly one hundred miles! Oh my God!" He'd tell me to go one step at a time, do the training, see how my body reacted, and go from there. This was the same strategy for any race—one step at a time. Break it up into digestible chunks and go from there.

So, when I got to the start line of TDS I felt strangely calm. I still wasn't sure how things would go, or if I was ready. But I knew that I had prepared the best I could, and I felt happy, strong, and confident that I could overcome any challenge that presented itself. I was stepping into the unknown, and I had practice doing that—every day since my accident two years previously. I was confident in my ability to problem-solve and overcome tough situations or the unexpected. Looking back, that was the training that really mattered.

The race didn't disappoint. Of course, it was hard, but I got through the low moments. I focused on what I could control and didn't lose sight of my goal: to finish and push as hard as I could. It was actually quite exciting. I was able to race the entire way; mere minutes separated the top three ladies for the majority of the day. I regained the lead at various points during the race, then lost it again, only to battle back and regain the lost time. I didn't give up.

Throughout the entire race, I remained within myself. I stayed positive, confident, happy. I crossed the finish line in second place, only ten minutes behind the leader—that's nothing over the course of a 145-kilometer race!

Crossing that finish line was one of the most magical experiences of my life. Every step of that race represented the progress I had made over the last two years. Every footstep was a testament to not giving up or giving in to what seemed impossible. Every rough patch I hit, I worked through, because I knew it would pass. I didn't give up; I couldn't let myself give up on my dreams.

When I finished the race, I looked back on the crowd in search of familiar faces. As I embraced my crew and reflected on everything I had felt that day, there was just one thing on my mind: belief.

That first month after my accident, broken and unable to move, I wrote this affirmation: "Believe. Believe that your best athletic days are ahead of you." That's when the tears came. I had carried that belief with me throughout the years, the lows, the setbacks, and on into this race day.

My journey is a testament to that belief. Never give up on something you love, something that's part of you, even when the journey is full of tears and obstacles. Keep holding on to it. Belief has the power to challenge the impossible.

ACKNOWLEDGMENTS

My story would not be possible without the support of a wonderful community of individuals near and far. I've mentioned many people throughout this book, and although I've left out many, those stories and memories are not forgotten.

I would like to extend a deep and sincere thank you to everyone who helped me in the early days of my recovery, and who continue to support me today. Recovery is an ongoing process, and I've realized that even a simple smile or conversation with a stranger can influence me in huge ways. Although thanking everyone is nearly impossible, I'd like to try my best to extend gratitude to those near to my heart.

I'll start with Manu Par. Without his bravery and instinctive actions, I wouldn't be here today. Thank you to those who were there during the rescue operation, including Martina Valmassoi, Ian Corless, Kilian Jornet, and the rescue team. Thank you to the team of Norwegian doctors and nurses who cared for me and operated on me; to Emelie Forsberg for calling my mother and keeping me company in the hospital room; to my team manager, Maeve Sloane, and The North Face for sending my mother to see me, and for hiring a private jet (with a very cute flight attendant) to help me get home to Colorado. Thank you to my sister, Gillian, who arranged all of my doctors' appointments and ordered all of my medical equipment (wheelchairs, scooters, and walkers, oh my!) for when I returned to Colorado. She and her husband, Scott, welcomed me into their home as I endured the first few weeks back in the U.S., and took care of me on top of having full-time jobs. Thank you to Allen Lim, and Rush Combs and Julia

German (and their dog, Hank!), for also letting me stay in their homes during this time and for doing so much to inspire me and support me during my time of recovery.

Thank you to Dave Mackey for his friendship and guidance. Thank you to Kelly Newlon for delivering wonderful, home-cooked meals to my doorstep. Thank you to Michelle Dziuban for constantly checking in on me, for meeting me for coffee, and for chauffeuring me around and encouraging me on those really low days. Thank you to Guy Love for giving me countless rides all over Boulder and the surrounding area, and never once complaining about it. Thank you to the incredible running community in Boulder, to Rocky Mountain Runners, and the running community as a whole—including the people I didn't even know—for mailing me care packages and letters, as well as leaving comments and messages on social media. You kept showing up for me and made me not want to give up on myself.

Thank you to Levi Younger, for his guidance and expertise in Rolfing, and for being a friend and confidant at a time when I was at my lowest. You gave me a safe place to express my fears (and many frustrations) and showed me it was possible to grow as an individual. You showed me how to let a helpless, negative experience shape me, teach me, and cultivate a positive perspective.

Thank you to my dear friend Lizi Bolanos-Nauth, whose constant positivity, vibrancy, and hard work were an example for me throughout my recovery. We might have met through injury, but it created an indestructible bond between us that will last a lifetime.

Thank you to Vince Heyd for doing laps with me on Grandeur Peak while I had a broken screw in my foot. Thank you for making me laugh while crying and for giving me hugs and encouragement during my first race back.

Thank you to my team at Revo Physiotherapy and Sports Performance, especially Matt Smith. Your guidance, both in physical rehab and mental fortitude, provided me with a plan to execute and a new hope to believe in.

Special thank you to my coach, Adam St. Pierre, who encouraged me, pushed me, and refused to give up on my dreams. You never stopped believing in me, even when my belief in myself was at an all-time low. You showed me what I was capable of and encouraged me to dream again. Thank you for your patience, guidance, encouragement, unyielding friendship, and support. I wouldn't be the athlete I am today without you.

A special thank you to my parents, who kept supporting me, even when I was a difficult person to love and support. Thank you especially to my mother, which goes without saying, but please let me try. You show me what it means to love unconditionally and what it means to follow your dreams and never give up on yourself. You are my example to follow. I continue to learn so much from you.

And finally, thank you to everyone who has continued to motivate me, encourage me, and inspire me at the later stages of my recovery and everywhere in between. Life is a never-ending journey of self-acceptance, growth, and discovery, with constant lessons in recovery, and it can't be done alone. Thank you to everyone who helped me along the way, big or small, both during my initial recovery and in the years that followed. Your impact has had lasting effects and requires my deepest gratitude.

ABOUT THE AUTHOR

Hillary Allen is from Fort Collins, Colorado. She grew up in an outdoorsy and scientific family who not only encouraged her to pursue a career in science, but also in sport. She earned a master's degree in neuroscience and physiology and structural biology from the University of Colorado Denver. During her graduate studies, Hillary also discovered trail running and ultrarunning. Her passion for the outdoors quickly led to success on the trails, and she became a sponsored mountain runner for The North Face. Along with her professional running and racing career, Hillary also teaches chemistry, biology, anatomy and physiology part-time at a small college outside of Boulder, Colorado. She also coaches other runners, again using her love of athletics and her physiology background.

MY RUNNING STATS

I first started running when I entered graduate school in 2011. I started with roads at first, joining a local running club and running three days a week. I didn't run particularly long distances at first, and it wasn't until a year later, December 2012, that I ran my first marathon: the California International Marathon, in 3:18:59. It was pouring rain that day and I was unsatisfied with my finishing time, so I ran one more self-supported marathon (measuring out the distance of a marathon by the number of loops around Washington Park in Denver, CO). I finished that run in 2:51:50.

Satisfied with my new time and ready for a new challenge—the trails—I ran my first ultramarathon in 2013: the Moab Red Hot 55km. My time wasn't that impressive; I walked most of it since I was unsure of how my body would hold up past the marathon mark. But after that race, something clicked, and the next year I really began to embrace ultrarunning. I started to discover my true potential on the trails, joined The North Face team, and began racing all over the world.

My racing style suited my nickname "Hillygoat" since I was choosing steep mountain races with extreme elevation gains and descents. A typical 50km (31m) race on this type of terrain could take over six hours. That time might not seem impressive, but if you factor in the elevation gain and loss (over 26,000 feet total—13,000 feet up and 13,000 feet down), it gives you a different perspective of how intense these types of races can be.

On the following pages I've shared a list of the races I have competed in all around the world. Take a look (especially at the elevation involved!) and you'll gain the same insight and admiration for these impressive mountain courses.

DATE	RACE	LOCATION	ELEVATION	FINISHING TIME	RANKING
6/23/2012	San Lorenzo River Trail Run 30k	Santa Cruz, CA	+/- 3,000 ft	2:53:53	3rd place, 6th overall
7/17/2012	Burton Creek Trail Run Half Marathon	Tahoe City, CA	+/- 1,500 ft	1:49:50	3rd place, 10th overall
2/16/2013	Moab Red Hot 55k	Moab, UT	+/- 5,115 ft	6:03:09	19th place, 101st overall
5/4/2013	Collegiate Peaks Trail Run 25m	Buena Vista, CO	+/-3 ,795 ft	3:45:53	2nd place, 25th overall
2/15/2014	Moab Red Hot 55k	Moab, UT	+/- 5,115 ft	4:52:01	3rd place, 25th overall
3/8/2014	Run Through Time Marathon	Salida, CO	+/- 4,785 ft (at altitude)	3:45:29	1st place, 22nd overall
4/26/2014	Cheyenne Mountain Trail Race 50k	El Paso County, CO	+/-6,600 ft	4:27:52	1st place (course record), 25th overall
6/19/2014	Bighorn Trail Run 52m	Big Horn, WY	+6,000 ft / -10,000 ft	8:56:39	1st place (course record), 3rd overall
7/19/2014	Speedgoat 50k	Snowbird Ski Resort, UT	+/- 12,210 ft	7:03:57	4th place, 36th overall
9/12/2014	Run the Rut 50k	Big Sky, MT	+/- 10,065 ft	7:00:31	5th place, 41st overall
10/4/2014	Flagstaff Sky Peaks 55k	Flagstaff, AZ	+/- 10,263 ft	6:46:05	1st place (course record), 9th overall
2014 U.S. SKYRUNNING ULTRA SERIES	2014 U.S. Skyrunning Competition	U.S. Skyrunning Ultramarathon Races			1st place, Ultra Series overall winner
3/7/2015	Way Too Cool 50k	Cool, CA	+/- 4,884 ft	4:15:53	12th place
5/30/2015	Quest for the Crest 50k	Burnsville, NC	+/- 11,253 ft	7:02:34	1st place (course record), 8th overall
6/26/2015	Marathon Du Mont-Blanc 80k	Chamonix, France	+/- 20,064 ft	13:11:40	3rd place, 22nd overall
7/25/2015	Speedgoat 50k	Snowbird Ski Resort, UT	+/- 11,600 ft	6:37:35	1st place (course record), 9th overall
9/5/2015	Run the Rut 50k	Big Sky, MT	+/- 10,065 ft	6:30:15	2nd place, 25th overall
10/1/2015	Festival des Templiers 78k	Millau, France	+/- 11,451 ft	9:09:26	12th place individual, Team USA 3rd place
2015 SKYRUNNER WORLD SERIES	2015 World Skyrunner Ultra Series	2015 World Skyrunner Ultra races			5th in the world ranking
5/7/2016	Transvulcania 73.5k	La Palma, Spain	+/- 14,058 ft	8:54:57	5th place
6/24/2016	Cortina Trail 48k	Cortina, Italy	+/- 8,712 ft	5:15:56	1st place (course record), 7th overall

DATE	RACE	LOCATION	ELEVATION	FINISHING TIME	RANKING
7/9/2016	Buff Epic Trail Aigüestortes 105k	Barruera, Spain	+/- 24,783 ft	15:40:06	5th place
9/4/2016	Run the Rut 50k	Big Sky, MT	+/- 10,065 ft	4:44:26	3rd place, 32nd overall
9/24/2016	Ultra Pirineu 110k	Bagà, Spain	+/- 21,120 ft	15:37:47	2nd place, 32nd overall
2016 SKYRUNNER WORLD SERIES	End-of-the-year championship award				2nd place
5/13/2017	Transvulcania 73.5k	La Palma, Spain	+/- 14,058 ft	8:38:46	3rd place, 42nd overall
6/3/2017	Madeira Skyrace 55k	Madeira, Portugal	+/- 15,114 ft	7:06:22	1st place (course record), 10th overall
6/24/2017	Olympus Marathon	Litochoro, Greece	+/- 10,791 ft	5:37:13	3rd place, 24th overall
7/8/2017	High Trail Vanoise 68k European Championships	Val d'Isère, France	+/- 16,830 ft	10:33:52	4th place, 23rd overall
8/5/2017	Tromsø Skyrace 57k	Tromsø, Norway	+/- 15,840 ft	DNF (did not finish)	
2017 SKYRUNNER WORLD SERIES	End-of-the-year championship award				2nd place
6/16/2018	The Broken Arrow Skyrace Vertical Kilometer	Olympic Valley, CA	+/- 2900 ft	46:28	2nd place, 12th overall
6/17/2018	The Broken Arrow Skyrace 52k (first Skyrace after injury)	Olympic Valley, CA	+/- 10,032 ft	6:08:21	6th place
6/23/2018	Cortina Trail 48k	Cortina, Italy	+/- 8,712 ft	5:19:20	1st place, 20th overall
10/10/2018	The North Face Endurance Challenge Chile 80k	Santiago, Chile	+/- 17,226 ft	11:52:07	1st place, 3rd overall
6/28/2019	Cortina Trail 48k	Cortina, Italy	+/- 8,712 ft	5:30:50	1st place, 23rd overall
7/21/2019	Royal Ultra Sky Marathon 55k (first World Series skyrace after accident)	Grand Paradiso, Italy	+/- 13,662 ft	9:44:53	11th place
8/3/2019	Tromsø Skyrace 57k	Tromsø, Norway	+/- 15,840 ft	10:09:11	11th place
8/28/2019	Ultra-Trail du Mont-Blanc TDS 145k	Courmayeur, Italy	+/- 30,129 ft	21:52:46	2nd place, 26th overall
10/12/2019	The North Face Endurance Challenge Chile 80k	Santiago, Chile	+/- 12,243 ft	9:36:36	1st place (course record), 5th overall